DARK MARKETS

PRINCETON LECTURES IN FINANCE

Yacine Aït-Sahalia, Series Editor

The Princeton Lectures in Finance, published by arrangement with the Bendheim Center for Finance of Princeton University, are based on annual lectures offered at Princeton University. Each year, the Bendheim Center invites a leading figure in the field of finance to deliver a set of lectures on a topic of major significance to researchers and professionals around the world.

Stephen A. Ross, *Neoclassical Finance*

William F. Sharpe, *Investors and Markets: Portfolio Choices, Asset Prices, and Investment Advice*

Darrell Duffie, *Dark Markets: Asset Pricing and Information Transmission in Over-the-Counter Markets*

Dark Markets

ASSET PRICING AND INFORMATION TRANSMISSION
IN OVER-THE-COUNTER MARKETS

Darrell Duffie

This work is published by arrangement with the
Bendheim Center for Finance of Princeton University

PRINCETON UNIVERSITY PRESS
PRINCETON AND OXFORD

Library of Congress Cataloging-in-Publication Data

Duffie, Darrell.
   Dark markets : asset pricing and information transmission in over-the-counter markets /
Darrell Duffie.
      p. cm.—(Princeton lectures in finance)
   Includes index.
   ISBN 978-0-691-13896-1 (hardcover : alk. paper) 1. Over-the-counter markets. 2. Capital
assets pricing model. I. Title.
   HG4521.D87 2012
   332.64'3—dc23

2011034092

British Library Cataloging-in-Publication Data is available

This book has been composed in Times
Printed on acid-free paper. ∞
Printed in the United States of America

1 3 5 7 9 10 8 6 4 2

To Kingston

Contents

Tables

Figures

Preface

This research monograph addresses the behavior of over-the-counter (OTC) markets. Rather than trading through a centralized mechanism such as an auction, specialist, or broadly accessible limit-order book, participants in an OTC market negotiate terms privately with other market participants, often pairwise. OTC investors, other than major dealers, may be largely unaware of prices that are currently available elsewhere in the market, or of recent transactions prices. In this sense, OTC markets are relatively opaque; investors are somewhat in the dark about the most attractive available terms and about who might offer them. We will focus attention on how prices, asset allocations, and information transmission in OTC markets are influenced by opaqueness.

The financial crisis of 2007–2009 brought significant concerns and regulatory action regarding the role of OTC markets, particularly from the viewpoint of financial instability. OTC markets for derivatives, collateralized debt obligations, and repurchase agreements played particularly important roles in the crisis and in subsequent legislation. The modeling of OTC markets, however, is still undeveloped in comparison to the available research on central market mechanisms.

My objective is to provide a brief introduction to OTC markets, including some of the key conceptual issues and modeling techniques. I hope to serve the interests of relevant sets of academics, investors, and regulators. Those reading beyond chapter 2 are assumed to have a graduate-level knowledge of probability theory.

Chapter 1 introduces the institutional setting of OTC markets and raises some of the key conceptual issues associated with market opaqueness. Chapter 2, from joint work with Adam Ashcraft, is a case example: the OTC market for overnight loans of federal funds, the "cash" of the U.S. banking system. Adam and I are grateful for support and data from the Federal Reserve Bank of New York and for conversations with Jamie McAndrews, Craig Furfine, and anonymous federal funds traders. We also benefited from comments by Andrew Metrick, Jeremy Stein, Ken French, Larry Harris, Owen Lamont, John Taylor, and Randy Westerfield. The views expressed in this chapter are not necessarily those of the Federal Reserve Bank of New York or the Federal Reserve System.

Chapter 3 familiarizes readers with the basic techniques used to model search and random matching in economies with many agents. The exact law of large numbers for random matching, stated rigorously in appendix A, is used to calculate the cross-sectional distribution of types of matches across the population. This is then extended to treat multiperiod search in both discrete-time and continuous-time frameworks. The optimal search intensity of a given agent, given the cross-sectional distribution of types in the population, is formulated and characterized with Bellman's principle. The chapter ends with a brief formulation of equilibrium search and a short review of the early history of the literature.

Chapter 4, from work by Duffie, Gârleanu, and Pedersen (2005, 2007), presents a simple introduction to asset pricing in OTC markets with symmetric information. Investors search for opportunities to trade and bargain with counterparties. Each of two negotiating investors is aware that a failure to complete a trade could lead to a potentially costly delay in order to search for a different counterparty. In equilibrium, the two investors agree to trade whenever there are potential gains from trade. The equilibrium asset price that they negotiate reflects the degree of search frictions, among other aspects of the market.

Chapter 5, based mainly on Duffie and Manso (2007), Duffie, Giroux, and Manso (2010), and Duffie, Malamud, and Manso (2010b), focuses on the "percolation" of information of common interest through an OTC market, as agents encounter each other over time and reveal information to each other, some of which they may have received earlier from other agents. The chapter includes an explicit solution of the evolution over time of the cross-sectional distribution in the population of the posterior probability assignments of the various agents.

Appendix A provides an exact law of large numbers for random matching, from Duffie and Sun (2007, 2011), which is relied upon in all of the theoretical chapters. Appendix B reviews the basics of counting processes with an intensity, such as Poisson processes.

The original impetus for this manuscript is the Princeton Lectures in Finance, given at Princeton University in late 2007. The title, "Dark Markets," was the result of a conversation with Yacine Aït-Sahalia, to whom I am also grateful for acting as my host for the Princeton lectures. Updated and enhanced versions of these lectures have been prepared for the 2008 Nash Lecture, hosted by Steven Shreve, at Carnegie-Mellon University; for a doctoral course at the University of Lausanne in the summer of 2009; for the Fields Institute Distinguished Lecture Series, April 2010, hosted in Toronto by Matheus Grasselli; for the Distinguished Lecture Series at Humboldt University hosted in Berlin by Ulrich Horst in June 2010; for the 2010 Tinbergen Lectures at the Duisenberg Institute, hosted in Amsterdam by André Lucas and Ton Vorst; and for the Minerva Foundation Lectures in the Mathematics Department at Columbia University in March 2011, hosted by Ioannis Karatzas and Johannes Ruf. I am grateful for many discussions with students and faculty during my visits to present these lecture series.

I am extremely grateful for research assistance from Sergey Lobanov, Felipe Veras, and Haoxiang Zhu. I have also had useful conversations with Pierre Collin-Dufresne, Alessio Farhadi, Kristoffer Laursen, Jason Granet, and Pierre-Olivier Weill. My largest debt is to my collaborators on this topic: Adam Ashcraft, Nicolae Gârleanu, Gaston Giroux, Semyon Malamud, Gustavo Manso, Lasse Heje Pedersen, Bruno Strulovici, Yeneng Sun, and Haoxiang Zhu. I have indicated throughout where I have drawn from our joint work. I am especially grateful for extensive comments provided on a prior version of the manuscript by Lasse Heje Pedersen, Felipe Veras, and two anonymous reviewers. I am also thankful to Janie Chan and Seth Ditchik of Princeton University Press for helpful editorial advice.

Darrell Duffie
Stanford University
May 2011

DARK MARKETS

CHAPTER 1

Over-the-Counter Markets

An over-the-counter (OTC) market does not use a centralized trading mechanism, such as an auction, specialist, or limit-order book, to aggregate bids
and offers and to allocate trades. Instead, buyers and sellers negotiate terms
privately, often in ignorance of the prices currently available from other potential counterparties and with limited knowledge of trades recently negotiated elsewhere in the market. OTC markets are thus said to be relatively
opaque; investors are somewhat in the dark about the most attractive available terms and about whom to contact for attractive terms. Prices and allocations in OTC markets are to varying extents influenced by opaqueness and
by the role of intermediating brokers and dealers. This chapter outlines some
of the key institutional features of OTC markets that influence the formation
of prices and allocations. Many details are omitted.

Some of the key research and policy issues regarding OTC markets include: (i) criteria that determine whether a financial product trades in an
OTC market or on an exchange, (ii) the manner in which the price negotiated on a particular trade reflects the relative degrees of connectedness of the
buyer and seller with the rest of the market, (iii) the formation and behavior
of dealer franchises and oligopolies as well as interdealer brokers, (iv) the
influence of market structure on the cross-sectional dispersion of prices negotiated at a particular time and on the time signature of price reactions to
supply or information shocks, (v) the evolution over time of the distribution
across investors of information learned from private trade negotiations, (vi)
the effect of pre-trade and post-trade price transparency on market behavior,
(vii) the impact of counterparty credit risk on pricing and financial stability, and (vii) the equilibrium strategies chosen by investors regarding their
search for counterparties. Some of these issues form the main subject matter
of this book. Others are left open for future research.

1.1   BILATERAL NEGOTIATION OF TERMS

Assets traded over the counter include most types of government and corporate bonds, asset-backed securities, securities lending and repurchase agreements, a wide range of derivatives, real estate, currencies, bulk commodities, shipping rights, and large blocks of equities. In most of these markets, trade is intermediated by dealers. Although the term "dealer" carries some legal distinctions in certain markets, the main difference between a dealer and other market participants is that, by convention, an OTC dealer is usually expected to make "two-way markets," in the following manner.

An OTC trade negotiation is typically initiated when an investor contacts a dealer and asks for terms of trade. Communication could be by phone, by e-mail, by screen-based query systems, or through a broker. A dealer making two-sided markets typically provides a take-it-or-leave-it pair of prices, a bid and an offer, to a customer. The customer may accept by immediately hitting the bid or lifting the offer. Dealer bids and offers are understood to be good for quantities up to an agreed conventional amount in standardized products. After agreeing on a price, a customer and dealer may further negotiate the quantity to be exchanged at the agreed price. Occasionally, if a customer declines to trade at the dealer's quotes, the dealer may offer a price concession rather than lose the opportunity to trade. In this case, the dealer is making a tradeoff between the value of maintaining a reputation for standing firm on its original quotes and the profit opportunity of the current trade.[1] A dealer trades for its own account and assumes the risk that it cannot offset a position at a profitable price.

An OTC bargaining game can be complex because of private information and the potentially rich sets of outside options of the respective counterparties. The counterparties may have different information regarding the common-value aspects of the asset (for example, the probability distribution of the asset's future cash flows), current market conditions, and their individual motives for trade. The counterparties may also be distinguished from each other with respect to their alternative trading opportunities, which depend on the manner and extent of their participation in the market. For

---

[1] A related reputation effect is explored by Atakan and Ekmekci (2010).

example, a dealer frequently negotiates trades and receives information, while the customer of a dealer usually has more limited opportunities to trade and thus relatively less information about recent transactions. Their different degrees of access to the market are in this case relatively common knowledge and tend to convey a negotiating advantage to the dealer. Beyond having more information than many of its customers, a dealer usually has less difficulty in adjusting inventories.[2] The negotiating advantage to a dealer may be increased when there are relatively few dealers with whom to negotiate. For example, as modeled by Zhu (2010), if an investor returns to a dealer from whom quotes have already been obtained, the dealer infers that the investor has had difficulty obtaining better terms from other dealers and is likely to offer even less attractive quotes to the investor.

Chapter 4 presents a simple model of the determination of prices in an OTC market with symmetric information. In this setting, prices reflect the fundamental values of the asset to the respective investors as well as the outside options of the respective counterparties to search for new trading partners. Chapter 5 focuses on the dynamics of asymmetric information across the population that is generated by OTC trading.

Some OTC markets have special intermediaries known as brokers that assist in negotiations between buyers and sellers, conveying the terms of one investor to another, usually without revealing the identities of the counterparties to each other. As opposed to dealers, a broker need not trade on its own account. Some brokers specialize in intermediating between dealers. A broker's customers rely on the broker for anonymity and for the broker's information regarding the most likely interested counterparties. Negotiation in OTC markets through brokers is often based on a "workup" protocol. Once the initial price and quantity are agreed on, one party can offer to expand the quantity of the trade. Further expansions can continue until at least one of the parties declines, although other parties in contact with the broker can then "enter" the trade at the same price, until no further trading interest is expressed at the original price, closing the trade. Huang, Cai, and Wang (2002), Boni and Leach (2004), and Pancs (2010) provide further description and analysis of the workup procedure and expandable-order markets.

---

[2] Inventory management by dealers and its implications for pricing are analyzed by Lyons (1995), O'Hara (1995), and Massa and Simonov (2003).

Over the past decade, the majority of interdealer and customer-to-dealer brokerage has moved to electronic platforms such as eSpeed, BrokerTec, Bloomberg, MarketAxess, MTS, and TradeWeb. Electronic trading platforms are likely to become more popular in OTC derivatives markets because of language in the U.S. Dodd-Frank Act of 2010 that mandates the trade of standardized OTC derivative products on a "swap execution facility" (SEF) that allows some degree of competition for trades among multiple market participants. As of this writing, the Securities and Exchange Comission (SEC) and the Commodity Futures Trading Commission (CFTC) have yet to define what will constitute an acceptable norm for SEFs. Once that is completed, perhaps in late 2011, the design of SEFs and the migration of trade in standardized OTC derivatives to SEFs will occur over time.

1.2   OTC TRANSPARENCY

In some dealer-based OTC markets, especially those with active brokers, a selection of recently quoted or negotiated prices is revealed to a wide range of market participants, often through electronic media such as Reuters, Bloomberg, or MarkitPartners. For other OTC markets, such as those for U.S. corporate and municipal bonds, regulators have mandated post-trade price transparency through the publication of an almost complete record of transactions shortly after they occur. In the United States, post-trade price reporting in many bond markets is done through the Trade Reporting and Compliance Engine (TRACE), which provides the price for each transaction within minutes of the trade. If the trade size is less than a stipulated threshold, TRACE reports the traded quantity. Otherwise, TRACE reports that the quantity was above the threshold. The size of extremely large trades is not publicly disclosed so that liquidity providers such as dealers have the chance to reduce inventory imbalances stemming from large trades with less concern that the size of a trade or their reservation price will be used to the bargaining advantage of their next counterparties.

In some active OTC derivatives markets, such as the market for credit default swaps, clients of dealers can request "dealer runs," which are essentially lists of dealers' prospective bid and offer prices on a menu of potential

trades. Dealers risk a loss of reputation if they frequently decline the opportunity to trade near these indicative prices when contacted soon after provid-
ing quotes for a dealer run.

Despite these sources of information, price transparency is typically
lower for OTC markets than for exchange-based markets, such as those
based on electronic communication networks (ECNs), in which there is essentially complete and immediate transactions reporting as well as pre-trade
transparency that includes at least the best executable bid and offer. The
complete contents of a typical ECN limit-order book are not normally disclosed. Some limit-order-book markets allow "icebergs," components of a
limit order that have undisclosed quantities. Those submitting icebergs may
wish to reduce inference by market participants that could worsen the order
submitter's ultimate average execution price.

Increasingly, investors can allocate orders to off-exchange "dark pools,"
where they are crossed at prices that were recently executed on exchanges.
Individual trades in dark pools are not normally disclosed. There has been
some concern that the increasing fraction of equity trades sent to dark pools
may lead to less competition for priced (on-exchange) trades and therefore
less market liquidity and price discovery. Zhu (2011) shows theoretical support, however, for a tendency of dark pools to be relatively heavily populated
by less informed traders. Under conditions, the presence of dark pools leads
to a higher concentration of more highly informed traders at "lit" exchanges,
which can actually improve price discovery.

The profits of a dealer depend on the volume of trade it handles and on
the average difference between bid and ask prices, which in turn depends
on the degree to which the dealer's customers are likely to have information
relevant to prices available elsewhere in the market. Dealers therefore pre-
fer at least some degree of market opaqueness. As pre-trade and post-trade
price transparency increases, dealers have incentives to narrow their bid-offer
spreads in order to compete for trading opportunities. If price transparency is
too great, however, some dealers may lose the incentive to intermediate, given
their fixed costs and the risk of adverse selection by informed customers. Unless the potential demand to trade a financial product is sufficient to justify
exchange trading, a sufficiently large increase in OTC market transparency
could therefore potentially reduce trading opportunities for investors.

Empirical anlyses of the implications of post-trade price transparency in bond markets, through TRACE, include those of Bessembinder and Maxwell (2008), Edwards, Harris and Piwowar (2007), Goldstein, Hotchkiss, and Sirri (2007), Green, Hollifield, and Schürhoff (2007a, 2007b), and Green, Li Schürhoff (2011). At this point, the empirical evidence does not generally support prior concerns expressed by dealers that the introduction of TRACE would reduce market liquidity.

The U.S. Dodd-Frank Act of 2010 regulates the transparency and stability of OTC derivatives markets in the United States. The European Commission plans to follow with its own new regulations. In addition to the impact on market transparency of mandated trade of standardized derivatives on swap execution facilities, the transparency requirements of the Dodd-Frank Act are of several major types: (i) the disclosure to regulators of all trade information through data repositories, (ii) the public disclosure of some aggregate information on trading volumes, and (iii) the public disclosure of transaction prices of standardized derivatives. The system for transaction price disclosure could be modeled on TRACE.

1.3   WHY TRADE OVER THE COUNTER?

Some of the lack of transparency of OTC markets is inherent in the nature of the underlying products. For example, a wide range of collateralized debt obligations and other structured credit products are thinly traded and have complex contractual features that could be analyzed well by only a narrow range of specialized investors. Even if such instruments were traded on an exchange, liquidity and transparency would be lacking. In any case, many such instruments could rarely achieve the volume and breadth of participation that would justify exchange-based trade. These are natural candidates for OTC trading, where customization of financial products to the needs of investors is more easily arranged. On request, an investment bank can offer a customer a new financial instrument for which there is no active market. In effect, an OTC market for that instrument is thereby created and may over time become established on the basis of additional trading. Eventually, if the product becomes sufficiently standardized and popular, its trade may migrate to an exchange.

Tufano (1989) describes the motivation of banks to innovate financial products. The introducer of a new financial product benefits in the short run from a temporary monopoly in the distribution of the product, through its command of the necessary technical and legal knowledge. Over time, a product may become sufficiently popular to encourage entry by other dealers. At this point, the original dealer's profit margins are likely to decline, although it may have a somewhat persistent advantage in terms of volume handled.

Some financial products with high volumes of trade that are relatively standard, for example, recently issued U.S. government bonds and certain liquid OTC derivatives (such as simple interest rate swaps and credit derivative index products), seem like natural candidates for exchange-based trade but are normally traded over the counter. At this point, we lack convincing theories that explain why such simple and heavily traded instruments are traded over the counter. Dealers have a vested interest in maintaining trade in OTC markets, where the profitability of intermediation is enhanced by market opaqueness. Once liquidity is established in OTC markets, it may be difficult for exchanges to compete for a critical mass of order flow, as investors are naturally drawn to the most liquid available market.

The prevalence of OTC trading for some standard financial products may be based in part on the granularity of trade sizes. Transactions of on-the-run government bonds, for instance, are often in quantities that are a substantial fraction of the total issuance size or daily volume of trade. A large quantity might be bought or sold at a more favorable price through private negotiation with a specialized OTC counterparty than by exposing the new demand or supply to a limit-order-book market populated by diversely motivated order submitters, where more severe price concessions may be required to digest a large position. For example, large block trades of equities are often executed in the private "upstairs" market of the New York Stock Exchange.[3] Her Majesty's Treasury reports an estimate by CREST, the United Kingdom's securities settlement system, that of the cash equity transactions placed into its system, OTC executions account for approximately 4% of the share volume and 14% of the market value of trades.[4]

---

[3] Keim and Madhavan (1996) analyze price formation in the upstairs search-based market for large blocks of equities.
[4] This does not not include equity transactions that are internalized over custodians' books or clearance services.

OTC derivatives and repurchase agreements, among certain other OTC bilateral contracts, expose each party of a trade to the risk that its counterparty will not perform as contracted, for example, because of bankruptcy. Even simple bank loans expose one of the two parties to the default risk of the other. If the default risk is not negligible, it is natural that the terms of these products are negotiated in the OTC market, so as to reflect the impact on each party of the default risk of the other. In OTC derivatives markets, the resulting price adjustment for counterparty default risk is called a credit value adjustment, or CVA.[5] It could be difficult to justify the cost of a distinct centralized market mechanism for derivatives that are materially exposed to the performance risk of an individual entity. A failure to price products according to the default risk of the specific counterparty invites adverse selection. For example, an offer to lend to a wide range of banks at a given interest rate leads to acceptance of the offer by borrowers with relatively high default risk. An attempt to correct for this adverse selection by raising the interest rate only worsens the credit quality of accepting borrowers. Anonymous exchange-based trading can therefore lead to inefficiently thin markets or even market failure.

1.4   MANAGING OTC CREDIT RISK

Techniques for mitigating OTC counterparty risk include the provision of collateral and, in some cases, central clearing. A financial contract is cleared when a special-purpose financial institution known as a central clearing party (CCP) becomes the buyer to the original seller, and the seller to the original buyer. By standing between the original parties to the trade, the CCP insulates each from the risk of default of the other, to the extent of the credit quality of the CCP itself.[6]

---

[5] Following the seminal paper of Sorensen and Bollier (1994), Duffie and Huang (1996) and Duffie, Schroder, and Skiadas (1996) modeled CVAs in settings in which the party at risk to default can change over time as the market value of the instrument to one of the two parties moves from positive to negative. This is typical of swap contracts.

[6] Duffie, Li, and Lubke (2009) review the central clearing of OTC derivatives among other policy issues regarding the infrastructure of OTC derivatives markets. Duffie and Zhu (2011) model the impact of clearing on counterparty credit risk and examine cases in which clearing is

Effectively designed and widely practiced central clearing improves the stability of the financial system by reducing the risk of chain-reaction failures of important financial institutions, and by lowering the incentives of investors to exit from positions with a financial institution whose solvency is suspected to be weak. These exits could contribute to a self-fulfilling "run" that reduces the liquidity of the weak financial institution to the point that it may indeed fail. CCPs can themselves be sources of inappropriately high systemic risk in the absence of sound CCP risk management, capital, collateral, regulatory supervision, and backstop sources of liquidity from lenders of last resort such as central banks.

The Dodd-Frank Act requires that standard derivatives traded by major market participants be cleared.[7] This legislation also mandates minimum collateral requirements, among other provisions.

1.5   PRICE BEHAVIOR WITH SEARCH FRICTIONS

There is extensive empirical evidence that supply or demand shocks in asset markets, in addition to causing an immediate price response, lead to adjustments over time in the distribution of capital across markets and adjustments over time in relative asset returns. In OTC markets, search delays could be responsible for some of these slow-recovery dynamics. Other causes of slow-recovery price dynamics are discussed by Duffie (2010). For modeling purposes, search could also proxy for other delays, such as those needed to establish trading relationships.

With delayed portfolio adjustments, there can be periods of time over which assets with essentially identical fundamental risks have different mean returns. More generally, there can be differences in mean returns across assets that are due not only to cross-sectional differences in "fundamental"

---

relatively ineffectual due to a potential loss of opportunities to net counterparty risk, which can happen with "too many" CCPs.

[7] The U.S. Treasury has proposed an exemption for foreign exchange derivatives that are settled by delivery of the two currencies. Duffie (2011) examines the foundation for this decision and provides a mechanism for obtaining the effect of clearing while leaving in place current processes for currency deliveries.

cash-flow risks but also to the degree to which the distribution of asset holdings across investors is inefficient (relative to a market without intermediation frictions). Empirical "factor" models of asset returns do not often
account for factors related to the distribution of ownership of assets or related to likely changes in the distribution of ownership.

For example, in OTC corporate bond markets, one observes large price
drops and delayed recovery in connection with major downgrades or defaults,
as described by Hradsky and Long (1989) and Chen, Lookman, Schürhoff,
and Seppi (2009), when certain classes of investors have an incentive or a
contractual requirement to sell their holdings.

Mitchell, Pedersen, and Pulvino (2007) document the effect on convertible bond hedge funds of large capital redemptions in 2005. Convertible
bond prices dropped and rebounded over several months. A similar drop-
and-rebound pattern was observed in connection was the LTCM collapse in
1998. Newman and Rierson (2003) show that large issuances of credit-risky
bonds temporarily raise credit spreads throughout the issuer's sector because
providers of liquidity such as underwriters, dealers, and hedge funds bear
extra risk as they search for long-term investors. They provide empirical
evidence of temporary bulges in credit spreads across the European Telecom debt market during 1999–2002 in response to large issues by individual
firms in this sector. Keim and Madhavan (1996) document analogous effects
in the upstairs search-based market for large blocks of equities.

The market for catastrophe risk insurance is characterized by price
surges, and then multiyear price declines, following sudden and large losses
of capital by insurers, for example, at times of major natural disasters, as
explained by Froot and O'Connell (1999). Periods of high insurance rates
are typically accompanied by new entrants into the market, including hedge
funds and other new insurers, whose capital has been mobilized by the high
risk premiums, but not immediately. It takes time to set up a viable new provider of catastrophe risk insurance.

The pricing of securities lending is relatively strongly connected to
search frictions, as explained by D'Avolio (2002), Duffie, Gârleanu, and
Pedersen (2002), Geczy, Musto, and Reed (2002), Porras Prado (2010), and
Blocher, Reed, and Van Wesep (2010).

In all of these examples, the time pattern of returns or prices after supply
or demand shocks reveals that the friction at work is not a transaction cost

for trade. If that were the nature of the friction, then all investors would immediately adjust their portfolios, or not, optimally, and the new market price and expected return would be immediately established and remain constant until the next change in fundamentals. In all of the above examples, however, after the immediate price response, whose magnitude reflects the size of the shock and the degree of short-term competition among investors who are immediately available to absorb the sudden supply or demand, there is a relatively lengthy period of time over which the price recovers somewhat (up after an adverse shock, down after a positive shock), reverting toward its new fundamental level. In the meantime, additional shocks can occur with overlapping consequences. The typical pattern suggests that the initial price response is larger than would occur with perfect capital mobility and reflects the demand curve of the limited pool of investors immediately available to absorb the shock. The speed of adjustment after the initial price response is a reflection, at least in part, of the time that it takes to contact and negotiate with additional investors.

A significant body of theory treats the implications of search frictions for asset pricing. Early search-based models of intermediation include those of Rubinstein and Wolinsky (1987), Bhattacharya and Hagerty (1987), Moresi (1991), Gehrig (1993), and Yavaş (1996). Differences in search frictions across different asset markets are treated by Vayanos and Wang (2007), Weill (2008), and Vayanos and Weill (2008). Duffie, Gârleanu, and Pedersen (2005) study search frictions in a single asset market with market making. Their work is extended by Lagos and Rocheteau (2009) to model heterogeneity in asset positions. Duffie, Gârleanu, and Pedersen (2007) and Lagos, Rocheteau, and Weill (2009) model the dynamics of prices in an asset market that are caused by a shock to the preferences of investors. Search frictions imply a gradual reallocation of the asset to the most suitable investors, as captured by a search-based asset-pricing model in chapter 4.

Duffie and Strulovici (2007) model the flow of capital from one asset market to another, seeking higher risk premia for the same risk, with intermediation at a search intensity that is endogenously chosen based on the rents that can be negotiated for intermediation, extending work by Weill (2007). In some parameterizations, search efforts go from minimal to maximal whenever the total amount of capital in one market is sufficiently low relative to that in another. Alternative approaches to modeling the implications for price dynamics of institutional frictions in capital movements are taken by Krishnamurthy and He (2010) and Gromb and Vayanos (2007).

In a relatively opaque OTC market, different investors may pay quite different prices for the same asset at essentially the same time. The investors may vary in terms of their relative bargaining power, their access to alternative trading opportunities, the quality of their information both about the fundamentals of the asset and about recent transactions.

For example, Green, Hollifield, and Schürhoff (2007a) document dramatic variation across investors in the prices paid for the same municipal bond. Massa and Simonov (2003) report dispersion in the prices at which different dealers trade the same Italian government bonds. In the next chapter, based on Ashcraft and Duffie (2007), we will see that the rate at which a pair of banks negotiate a loan of federal funds in the overnight interbank market at a given time of day, relative to the average rate negotiated by other pairs of banks at the same time of day, varies according to the relative cash holdings of the two banks at that moment of the day, the degree to which the two banks are active in the interbank lending market, and the extent to which the banks have had a prior borrower-lender relationship, among other factors.

CHAPTER 2

The Case of Federal Funds Lending

This chapter[1] shows how the intraday allocation and pricing of overnight loans of federal funds reflect the OTC interbank market in which these loans are traded. A would-be borrower or lender typically finds a counterparty institution by direct bilateral contact. Once in contact, say by telephone, the two counterparties to a potential trade negotiate terms that reflect their incentives for borrowing or lending, as well as the attractiveness of their respective options to forego a trade and to continue "shopping around." This OTC pricing and allocation mechanism is quite distinct from that of most centralized markets, such as an electronic limit-order-book market in which every order is anonymously exposed to every other order with a centralized order-crossing algorithm. Afonso and Lagos (2011) have developed supporting theory.

Among other new empirical results, this chapter provides estimates of how the likelihood that some bank i borrows from some other bank j during a particular minute t of a business day, as well as the interest rate on the loan, depend on the prior trading relationship between these two banks, the extents to which their balances at the beginning of minute t are above or below their normal respective balances for that time of day, their overall levels of trading activities, the amount of time left until their end-of-day balances are monitored for reserve-requirement purposes, and the volatility of the federal funds rate in the trailing 30 minutes.

While there is a significant body of research on the microstructure of specialist and limit-order-book markets, most OTC markets do not have

[1] This chapter, joint work with Adam B. Ashcraft, is a revised and extended version of Ashcraft and Duffie (2007), which appeared in 2007 as "Systemic Illiquidity in the Federal Funds Market" in *American Economic Review, Papers and Proceedings*, vol. 97, pp. 221–225. The views expressed here are not necessarily those of the Federal Reserve Bank of New York or the Federal Reserve System.

comprehensive transactions-level data available for analysis. The federal funds market is a rare exception. We go beyond the seminal study by Furfine (2001) of the microstructure of the federal funds market by modeling how the likelihood of matching a particular borrower with a particular lender, as well as the interest rate they negotiate, depend on their respective incentives to add or reduce balances and their abilities to conduct further trading with other counterparties (proxied by the level of their past trading volumes). Our results are consistent with the thrust of search-based OTC market theories described in chapters 4 and 5.

2.1   THE FEDERAL FUNDS MARKET

Federal funds are deposits, denominated in U.S. dollars, held at Federal Reserve Banks ("the Fed") by regulated financial institutions. Essentially, federal funds are the cash of the U.S. interbank market.

Federal funds can be transferred from one U.S. regulated financial institution to another with an electronic request by the sending financial institution to the Fed via its Fedwire Funds Service. The sender's instruction is to debit its own federal funds account by a stipulated amount in favor of the account of the receiving institution. Such a "send" transaction could occur for many purposes, for example, to fund or repay a loan of federal funds or as settlement of a trade for other assets.

The normal terms of a federal funds loan are the amount and the interest rate, quoted on a simple overnight money-market (actual-360) basis. Overnight loans, the focus of this chapter, are to be repaid by 6:30 p.m. Eastern time on the next business day. For example, a loan of $100 million at a rate of 7.20% on a Tuesday would be executed with a send by the lender to the borrower of $100 million on Tuesday and a send by the borrower to the lender of $100(1 + 0.072/360) = \$100.02$ million on Wednesday. (For a Friday-to-Monday loan, the repayment with three days of interest would be $100.06 million.)

Federal funds loans are not collateralized and therefore expose the lending institution to the risk of default by the borrowing institution. Credit risk could be partly responsible for the OTC structure of the federal funds market.

Not every loan is of the same quality. The willingness of the lender to expose itself to a particular borrower and a determination of the interest rate on the loan would be awkward to arrange in a typical centralized order-processing market of the sort that normally handles homogeneous assets.

Two financial institutions can come into contact with each other by various methods in order to negotiate a loan. For example, a federal funds trader at one bank could telephone a federal funds trader at another bank and ask for quotes. The borrower and lender can also be placed in contact through a broker, although the final amount of a brokered loan is arranged by direct negotiation between the borrowing and lending banks. With our data, described in the next section, we are unable to distinguish which loans were brokered. In aggregate, approximately 27% of the volume of federal funds loans during our 2005 sample period were brokered.[2] Based on our conversations with market experts, we believe that brokerage of loans is less common among the largest banks, which are the focus of our study.

With rare exception, any institution's federal funds balance must be nonnegative at the close of every business day. If necessary, the discount window is available as a backstop source of federal funds loans directly from the Fed. Loans through the discount window, however, are at an interest rate that was set during our data period at 100 basis points above the current targeted federal funds rate. The discount window rate is therefore highly unattractive to a trader that might have been able to borrow directly from another market participant at rates that are typically negotiated within a few basis points of the target rate. A loan from the discount window, moreover, must be collateralized by acceptable assets that are supplied to the Fed by the borrowing financial institution. This constitutes another incentive to achieve nonnegative balances without using the discount window.

Regulated U.S. depository institutions are required to hold federal reserves, comprised of paper currency inventories and federal funds deposits, in minimum amounts relative to the institution's trailing average level of deposits, as explained by Hamilton (1996). A bank's reserves are monitored by the Fed every two weeks. Federal funds deposits are adjusted as needed

---

[2] This figure comes from the Payments Studies Function of the Federal Reserve Bank of New York and is calculated by combining several data sources.

by the bank in order to meet its average daily reserve requirements. Leading up to the financial crisis of 2007–2009, large banks typically targeted rather small positive balances relative to the total amounts they sent over Fedwire. In 2006, for example, the average total amount of reserves held daily by financial institutions was roughly $17.3 billion, whereas the average daily total amount sent on Fedwire was over $2.3 trillion. Banks did not have much incentive to hold reserve balances in large amounts at the close of business days because these balances did not earn interest from the Fed during our data period. (The Fed began paying interest on federal funds deposits in the course of the financial crisis of 2007–2009.) During our sample period, large banks therefore had a significant incentive near the end of each day to exchange any unnecessary balances of federal funds for interest-bearing overnight assets such as commercial paper or reverse repurchase agreements. Banks economized on holdings of federal funds through the use of "sweep" accounts, in which customer funds held as demand deposits during the day are "swept" into money-market accounts at the end of each day, thereby increasing the interest earnings of customers and reducing the quantity of reserves a bank was required to hold. The resulting small total amount of reserves held by banks relative to the demand for federal funds transactions conveyed some advantage to the Fed in targeting interest rates though open-market transactions because adding or removing a relatively small amount of reserves from the system had a significant proportionate influence on the scarcity of reserves available as a medium of exchange for intraday transactions and for purposes of meeting reserve requirements.

During the business day, financial institutions are permitted to have negative balances in their accounts up to a regulatory cap. Beyond the cap, these "daylight overdrafts" are charged a penalty fee.[3]

During the financial crisis of 2007–2009, the Fed dramatically increased the amount of federal funds held by banks through "quantitative easing," that is, by creating new federal funds in order to purchase securities from banks. In so doing, the Fed mitigated the severity of the financial crisis. During the

---

[3] Because of precrisis increases in daylight overdrafts, regulators discussed the informal practice by some market participants of offering lower interest rates on loans that are for return early on the next business day. See Johnson (2006).

financial crisis, the Fed also began paying interest to banks on their deposits of federal funds. Because of these actions by the Fed, quantitative easing and paying interest on federal funds, most banks had reduced incentives to closely manage their intraday balances of federal funds. As a result, search frictions became much less important. Our precrisis data are therefore fortuitous from the viewpoint of examining the impact of search frictions on market behavior.

Motivated in part by our discussions with federal funds traders, we document that during our data period federal funds trading behavior was significantly more sensitive to balances during the last hour of the day. Consistent with the importance of controlling end-of-day balances, federal funds traders at some large banks arranged for other profit centers of their banks to avoid large unscheduled transactions involving federal funds (for example, currency trades) near the end of each day. Once a federal funds trader has a reasonable estimate of the day's yet-to-be-executed send and receive transactions, he or she can adjust rate quotes and pursue trading opportunities with other banks so as to push the bank's balances in the desired direction. We show evidence of this behavior and further find that lending is more active when federal funds rate volatility in the trailing half-hour is high.

Hamilton (1996) discusses the implications of the two-week monitoring cycle for daily price behavior. We do not find evidence of significant dependence of intraday balance targeting on the number of days remaining in the current two-week monitoring period.

We do not consider behavior on days of extreme stress, such as the stock market crash of 1987 or on September 11, 2001, when the events at the World Trade Center prevented the Bank of New York from being able to process payments. Access to the discount window and massive infusions of liquidity by the Fed and other central banks would (and did, on 9/11) mitigate adverse systemic effects, as explained by McAndrews and Potter (2001) and Lacker (2004).

2.2   DATA

This study uses transactions-level data from Fedwire. We focus mainly on the top 100 commercial banks by transaction volume and on the business days of 2005. Our data permit the construction of real-time balances for each institution and allow us to identify the sender and receiver of both payments and loans.

We start with payments data that include every transaction sent over Fedwire during the 251 business days of 2005. These data include the date, time, amount, and account numbers involved in each transaction. We focus on transactions in the last 90 minutes of the Fedwire business day, between 5:00 p.m. and 6:30 p.m. Eastern time. The large institutions that we study frequently have multiple accounts. We aggregate these accounts by institution, using a mapping from accounts to institutions that is updated every month. We restrict our sample to institutions that are either commercial banks or government-sponsored enterprises (GSEs) such as Freddie Mac, Fannie Mae, and Federal Home Loan Banks. We eliminated transactions involving accounts held by central banks, federal or state governments, or other settlement systems. Using these data, we identify the top 100 institutions in each month by the total dollar volume sent, which ranges from less than \$4 billion to more than \$2 trillion. The median monthly volume of federal funds sent across the 1200 institution-months in our sample is \$19.21 billion. The median across months of the aggregate volume sent is \$12.46 trillion. Over 80% of the institution-months in our sample are for commercial banks, 15% are for GSEs, and the remaining 5% are for special situations (nonbanks that hold reserve balances at the Federal Reserve). Because our analysis is done at the level of financial institutions rather than accounts, we remove all transactions for which the same institution is the sender and receiver. For purposes of modeling transaction events, we aggregate transactions by date for each sender-receiver pair (of the $9900 = 100 \times 100 - 100$ pairs) for each of the minutes of the last 90 minutes of the business day. For example, if bank i sends to bank j twice during the minute spanning 17:45 to 17:46, we treat this as one event.

We use a data set designed by the Payments Studies Function at the Federal Reserve Bank of New York to identify as likely loans those transactions that involve a send in denominations of \$1 million between a pair of counterparties that is reversed the following business day with plausible federal funds interest. These data are merged with our Fedwire send data in order to separate federal funds loans from nonloan sends. We also use a data set that documents the balance of each account at the end of every minute in which a transaction occurs. These balances are aggregated across all accounts for each institution, giving us each institution's account balance for each of the last 90 minutes of every business day in our sample. In order to deal with heterogeneity across institutions and time, we normalize each institution's account balance by the following method. From the account balance of institution i at minute t on a particular day, we subtract the median balance for institution i at minute t across all 251 business days of 2005. We then divide this difference by the total amount V_i of federal funds sent by this institution over the last 90 minutes of the day in the current month. This normalized balance, denoted $X_i(t)$, is a measure of the extent to which institution i has more or less than its normal balance for that minute relative to the size of the institution (measured by transactions volume).

Among our other explanatory variables are measures of the volatility of the federal funds rate and of the strength of the relationship between pairs of counterparties. In order to capture the volatility of the federal funds rate, we start with a dollar-weighted average during a given minute t of the interest rates of all loans made in that minute. We then measure the time-series sample standard deviation of these minute-by-minute average rates over the previous 30 minutes, denoted $\sigma(t)$. The median federal funds rate volatility is about 3 basis points but ranges from under 1 basis point to 87 basis points with a sample standard deviation of 4 basis points. Our measure of sender-receiver relationship strength for a particular pair (i, j) of counterparties, denoted S_{ij}, is the dollar volume of transactions sent by i to j over the previous month divided by the dollar volume of all transactions sent by i to the top 100 institutions. The receiver-sender relationship strength R_{ij} is the dollar volume of transactions received by i from j over the previous month divided by the dollar volume of all transactions received by i from the top 100 institutions. Because we use a 1-month-lagged measure of relationship strength, we do not include transactions from the first month of 2005.

2.3   ANALYSIS OF TRANSACTION-PAIRING LIKELIHOOD

We begin with an analysis of the determinants of the likelihood $p_{ij}(t)$ of a loan (or of a nonloan send) by institution i to institution j during minute t of a particular business day. We separately analyze loan transactions and non-loan sends. Separate logit models are estimated for each business day. The estimated probability that institution i sends (or lends) to institution j during minute t is modeled with variants of the logit model

$$p_{ij}(t) = \Lambda(1, V_i, V_j, X_i(t), X_j(t), S_{ij}, R_{ij}, \sigma(t), L(t); \beta), \qquad (2.1)$$

where, for a vector x of covariates and a vector β of coefficients,

$$\Lambda(x; \beta) = \frac{e^{\beta \cdot x}}{1 + e^{\beta \cdot x}},$$

and where $L(t)$ is the indicator variable (1 or 0) for whether t is after 17:30 Eastern time. (The covariate 1 allows for a constant term in the list of covariates.)

Table 2.1 shows summary statistics for the maximum likelihood estimate of the coefficient vector $\hat{\beta}$ of (2.1) and of variants of (2.1) that include interactions of some of the explanatory variables with the late-time indicator $L(t)$. Rather than reporting the coefficients separately for each business day, Table 2.1 reports, for each of the models labeled (a)–(f), the mean across business days of the estimated coefficients and of the associated t-statistics, as well as the mean absolute deviation across days of the coefficient estimates and of the t-statistics. There are enough data on each business day to identify the coefficients well on most days, and we are reluctant to pool the data across business days because of nonstationarity concerns. Indeed, the estimated coefficients do vary substantially across business days but are typically statistically significantly different than zero at standard confidence levels. The first and third rows of model (a) in table 2.1 document a strong relationship between counterparty balances and the probability of a federal funds loan. A high balance relative to normal for that minute increases the probability of being a lender to a particular potential counterparty. A low balance increases the probability of being a borrower. The second and fourth rows of model (a) show that this relationship tends to be much stronger during the last 60 minutes of the day. Comparing the estimated coefficients for loans with those for nonloan sends in model (d), we surmise that the likelihood of a loan is more sensitive to balances than is the likelihood of a nonloan send. For instance, a bank in need of federal funds would be more likely to increase

Table 2.1 Logit Models of Transaction Likelihood

	Federal Funds Loans						Nonloan Sends					
	(a)		(b)		(c)		(d)		(e)		(f)	
	$\hat{\beta}$	t-stat	$\hat{\beta}$	t-stat	$\hat{\beta}$	t-stat	$\hat{\beta}$	t-stat	$\hat{\beta}$	t-stat	$\hat{\beta}$	t-stat
1. $X_s(t)$	16.73 (9.36)	7.98 (4.75)	-2.46 (31.60)	0.66 (3.83)	16.32 (7.87)	6.01 (3.02)	-1.46 (7.23)	-2.28 (11.27)	-4.04 (14.60)	-0.90 (3.58)	-0.93 (6.44)	-1.52 (9.42)
2. $X_s(t)L(t)$	26.77 (12.54)	7.33 (3.11)	23.95 (14.71)	4.89 (2.85)	28.07 (13.46)	6.07 (2.53)	1.27 (12.08)	1.39 (6.06)	1.18 (10.18)	1.05 (4.66)	1.27 (11.98)	1.19 (5.67)
3. $X_r(t)$	-9.37 (9.57)	-3.32 (3.85)	15.61 (37.89)	0.91 (2.60)	-7.09 (8.21)	-2.32 (2.73)	-2.15 (6.57)	-3.69 (10.91)	-1.71 (11.42)	-0.59 (3.16)	-1.50 (5.45)	-2.64 (8.71)
4. $X_r(t)L(t)$	-26.69 (16.34)	-4.37 (2.56)	-21.55 (18.54)	-3.06 (2.55)	-24.72 (15.16)	-3.89 (2.27)	-0.86 (9.72)	-0.59 (5.37)	-0.54 (8.30)	-0.30 (4.10)	-0.54 (8.81)	-0.36 (4.84)
5. $L(t)$	-0.87 (0.15)	-10.54 (1.69)	-0.66 (0.29)	-7.10 (3.40)	-0.85 (0.14)	-9.67 (1.50)	-1.44 (0.08)	-64.71 (3.18)	-1.11 (0.40)	-45.06 (19.01)	-1.45 (0.08)	-63.57 (3.08)
6. V_s	0.92 (0.05)	32.98 (2.04)	0.92 (0.05)	33.00 (2.06)	0.68 (0.05)	21.45 (1.78)	0.71 (0.02)	114.52 (5.96)	0.71 (0.02)	114.33 (5.90)	0.51 (0.03)	68.99 (4.31)
7. V_r	0.87 (0.04)	33.79 (2.35)	0.87 (0.04)	33.87 (2.31)	0.58 (0.04)	21.46 (1.75)	0.62 (0.02)	103.18 (5.28)	0.62 (0.02)	103.19 (5.22)	0.43 (0.02)	62.47 (3.61)
8. $X_s(t)\sigma(t)$			8.45 (12.82)	2.68 (3.69)					1.34 (6.00)	0.77 (3.62)		
9. $X_r(t)o(t)$			-10.73 (15.52)	-2.22 (2.74)			-0.32	0.02	(4.56)	(2.81)		
10. $\sigma(t)$			-0.27 (0.25)	-5.01 (3.08)			-0.44	-25.92	(0.40)	(17.61)		
11. S_{sr}					3.13 (0.24)	19.86 (1.80)					1.70 (0.09)	24.32 (1.35)
12. R_{rs}					2.76 (0.20)	20.93 (2.12)					1.93 (0.13)	22.73 (2.16)
13. constant	-52.08 (2.29)	-43.35 (2.47)	-51.60 (2.24)	-42.87 (2.55)	-38.80 (1.78)	-33.66 (2.23)	-36.79 (1.10)	-150.92 (7.00)	-35.95 (1.30)	-143.84 (7.88)	-26.93 (1.12)	-92.74 (4.96)

The table summarizes the fit of six logit models, labeled (a)–(f), for the probability of a loan (models (a)–(c)) or of a nonloan send (models (d)–(f)) in minute t. Each model is estimated separately for each of the business days of the last 11 months of 2005. Each day has 891,000 = $(100 \times 100 - 100) \times 90$ observations, one for each sender-receiver-minute combination for the top 100 institutions over the last 90 minutes of the business day. For each covariate, the table reports the mean across days of the maximum likelihood estimate of the coefficients and of the corresponding t-statistics. The second row, for each covariate, shows the mean absolute deviation across all business days of the estimated coefficients and of the corresponding t-statistics.

its borrowings than to increase its sales of other assets such as treasuries or currencies.

Row 5 in table 2.1 indicates that the probabilities of loans and of nonloan sends decline as the business day comes to a close. Rows 6 and 7 are evidence of the unsurprising fact that larger institutions are much more likely to be counterparties on all types of transactions. Related to this, Craig and von Peter (2010) provide evidence of the degree to which interbank Euro loans in Europe are tiered, with smaller banks having relationships with larger banks. This is consistent with our U.S. data and with the work of Soromäki, Bech, Arnold, Glass and Beyeler (2007).

The coefficient estimates of rows 8 and 9 indicate that an increase in funds rate volatility increases the probability of lending and reduces the probability of borrowing but has little effect on the probability of sending or receiving. From row 10, higher funds rate volatility tends to depress lending and sending, although it seems to have a larger impact on the latter. Finally, rows 10 and 11 document that relationship strength has a significant impact on lending or sending, although this effect is much larger for lending than for sending.

2.4   DETERMINANTS OF THE RATE

We are interested in an understanding of the determinants of cross-sectional variation, at a given minute t, of the rate $r_{ij}(t)$ negotiated by a particular lender i and borrower j, net of the current-minute dollar-weighted average rate $R(t)$ negotiated elsewhere in the market. Our rate data are those for all federal funds loan transactions made between our top 100 institutions during 2005. As explanatory variables, we consider the cross-sectional deciles d_i^b and d_j^b of the lender's and borrower's normalized balances $X_i(t)$ and $X_j(t)$, respectively, relative to the population at minute t. The highest-decile institutions (with $d_i^b = 90$) are likely to be among those whose incentive to lend is greatest, other effects equal. In a centralized market, any market order is assigned the best available price. In an OTC market, however, theory suggests that the price negotiated is increasing in the reservation prices of the buyer and the seller. Our explanatory variable for this effect in the federal funds market is the sum $d_i^b + d_j^b$ of the percentile balances of the lender

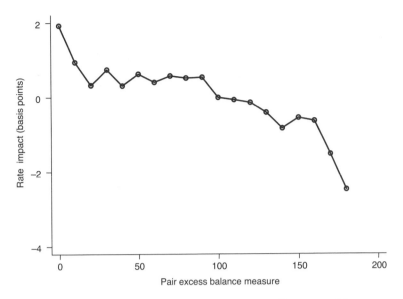

Figure 2.1: Dependence of rate on borrower and lender balances. The average of the rate negotiated, relative to the mean market rate at that minute, depends on the sum of the excess-balance
percentiles of the borrower and lender banks before controlling for other determinants.

and the borrower. We anticipate that $r_{ij}(t) - R(t)$ decreases, on average, with
$d_i^b + d_j^b$. The results of our panel regression of rates is anticipated by figure
2.1, which shows that the rate negotiated indeed declines with the sum of the
excess-balance percentiles of the borrower and lender before controlling for
other determinants of the rate.

A significant number of loans in our data are made by lenders whose relative balances are in the lower deciles of the sample. Many of these lenders
are presumably themselves in relative need of funds but agree to lend at a
sufficiently high rate, planning to borrow later in the day at a lower rate. In
an OTC market, the borrower does not generally know the most attractive
rates available from other counterparties, nor which counterparties are offering them, and may have an incentive to accept the rate offered by such
a lender. The alternative is to shop around for better terms, which involves
delay and effort. The delay could be more costly near the end of the day.
More active institutions are in a better position to offer loans when in need
of funds themselves because they are in a relatively good position to raise

their inventory of federal funds before the end of the day. An analogous effect applies to institutions who are willing to borrow despite having excess balances. We estimate the impact of these effects on the rate negotiated by including as an explanatory variable the difference $d_i^v - d_j^v$ between the cross-sectional decile d_i^v of the lender's transaction volume V_i and the corresponding decile d_j^v of the borrower. By theory, we expect that $r_{ij}(t) - R(t)$ increases on average with $d_i^v - d_j^v$.

In order to account for the ability of federal funds traders to forecast their nonloan sends and receipts during the remainder of the day, we also construct a proxy for the conditional expectation at time t of the end-of-day balance of a given institution in the absence of any additional borrowing and lending after time t. This proxy is the current balance plus all net nonloan sends for the remainder of the day. The true conditional expectation differs from this outcome proxy by an amount uncorrelated with information available at the forecast time. The regressor that we use is the sum of the cross-sectional percentiles of this balance-outcome proxy for the lender i and borrower j, again labeled $d_i^b + d_j^b$. We also include as a regressor the interaction of $d_i^b + d_j^b$ with the dummy variable $L(t)$ for the last hour of the business day.

Table 2.2 documents the estimated coefficients, above the standard errors, for each of models (a)–(h), whose dependent variable is $r_{ij}(t) - R(t)$ and whose regressors are indicated. Models (a)–(d) use actual balances to determine d_i^b, whereas models (e)–(h) use our outcome proxies for conditional expected balances. For models (a), (c), (e), and (g), the market rate $R(t)$ is the dollar-weighted average rates on all other loans at the same minute t. For models (b), (d), (f), and (h), the market rate $R(t)$ is measured by regressing the actual rates negotiated on date and time-of-day dummies.

The first two rows in table 2.2 document that, on average during the last hour of the day, increasing the balances of the lender and borrower does indeed reduce the loan interest rate that they negotiate relative to rates negotiated elsewhere in the market during the same minute. The third row shows that, on average, the rate negotiated is higher for lenders who are more active in the federal funds market relative to the borrower. Likewise, if the borrower is more active in the market than the lender, the rate negotiated is lower, other things equal. The fourth row documents that this effect is stronger during the last hour of the day.

Table 2.2 OLS Models of the Loan Rates

	Actual Balance				Expected Balance			
	(a)	(b)	(c)	(d)	(e)	(f)	(g)	(h)
1. $d_z^b + d_r^b$	0.0024**	0.0040***	0.0027***	0.0044***	0.0017	0.0021	0.0021*	0.0025
	(0.0010)	(0.0011)	(0.0010)	(0.0011)	(0.0012)	(0.0017)	(0.0012)	(0.0018)
2. $(d_s^b + d_r^b)L(t)$	−0.0260***	−0.1049***	−0.0266***	−0.1061***	−0.0011	−0.0086***	−0.0016	−0.0094**
	(0.0053)	(0.0068)	(0.0053)	(0.0068)	(0.0031)	(0.0043)	(0.0030)	(0.0043)
3. $d_z^v + d_r^v$	0.0137**	0.0205***			0.0136**	0.0202***		
	(0.0066)	(0.0076)			(0.0066)	(0.0077)		
4. $(d_s^v + d_r^v)L(t)$	0.0691***	0.0696***			0.0742***	0.0907***		
	(0.0085)	(0.0079)			(0.0085)	(0.0085)		
5. S_{sr}	0.3548	0.9753	0.2092	0.7839	0.3667	0.9496	0.2235	0.7621
	(1.5936)	(1.5033)	(1.5191)	(1.4122)	(1.5924)	(1.5118)	(1.5179)	(1.4206)
6. R_{sr}	3.1219**	2.5496**	2.8965**	2.3494**	3.1021**	2.4962*	2.8730**	2.2831**
	(1.3213)	(1.2897)	(1.1907)	(1.1171)	(1.3232)	(1.3090)	(1.1925)	(1.1348)
7. d_s^v			0.0212***	0.0293***			0.0211***	0.0291***
			(0.0073)	(0.0086)			(0.0073)	(0.0086)
8. d_r^v			0.0063	0.0039			0.0064	0.0043
			(0.0077)	(0.0081)			(0.0077)	(0.0082)
9. $d_s^v L(t)$			0.0750***	0.0870***			0.0799***	0.1066***
			(0.0103)	(0.0112)			(0.0103)	(0.0117)
10. $d_r^v L(t)$			−0.0653***	−0.0470***			−0.0711***	−0.0711***
			(0.0122)	(0.0159)			(0.0123)	(0.0166)
No. observations	121,189	123,236	121,189	123,236	121,189	123,236	121,189	123,236
R^2	0.02	0.03	0.02	0.04	0.02	.02	0.02	0.02

The table summarizes the OLS estimates of the coefficients of various models of the funds rate, labeled (a)–(h) by column. The underlying data include all federal funds loans made in 2005 between the top 100 institutions defined by total send volume each month. Regressors include the decile d_s^b of the balance of the lender at the time of the loan plus decile d_r^b of the balance of the borrower at the time of the loan; the interaction of the previous variable with $L(t)$; the deciles d_s^v and d_r^v of the gross federal funds transactions of the lender and borrower in the previous month, respectively; the interaction of the previous variables with $L(t)$; and a full set of time-of-day fixed effects. Models (a)–(d) are based on the actual balance of the counterparties; models (e)–(h) are based on the forecasted balances of the counterparties. For each regressor of each model, the table reports the estimated coefficient above the standard error, which has been corrected for heteroskedasticity and clustering at the sender-receiver level using the Stata robust cluster options.

In order to mitigate concerns that size is a proxy for credit risk, models (c), (d), (f), and (h) include the lender and borrower size deciles as separate regressors. The results show that most of the impact of size on rate is associated with the lender size, which has no direct bearing on the credit quality of the borrower. For empirical models of how credit quality affects interbank loan rates, see Cocco, Gomes, and Martins (2009) and Furfine (2001).

In a separate analysis of our data, we have also verified that agency credit ratings[4] of the borrower, for the subset of borrowers that we considered, played a statistically significant role in the interest rate granted on the loan but with a magnitude much smaller than that associated with the other effects we have described. During the financial crisis of 2007–2009, however, especially around the time of the failure of Lehman Brothers, interbank loan rates varied much more substantially across borrowers based on concerns about credit quality.

---

[4] As a matter of disclosure, since completing this study, I became a member of the board of directors of Moody's Corporation, which operates a major rating agency.

CHAPTER 3

Search for Counterparties

This chapter introduces the modeling of search and random matching in large economies. The objective is to build intuition and techniques for later chapters. After some mathematical prerequisites, the notion of random matching is defined. The law of large numbers is then invoked to calculate the cross-sectional distribution of types of matches. This is extended to multiperiod search, first in discrete-time settings and then in continuous time. The optimal search intensity of a given agent, given the cross-sectional distribution of types in the population, is characterized with Bellman's principle. We then briefly take up the issue of equilibrium search efforts.

3.1 PRELIMINARIES

We fix some mathematical preliminaries, beginning with a probability space $(\Omega, \mathcal{F}, \mathbb{P})$. The elements of Ω are the possible states of the world. The elements of $\mathcal{F}$ are events, sets of states to which we can assign a probability. The probability measure $\mathbb{P}$ assigns a probability in $[0, 1]$ to each event. We also fix a measure space $(G, \mathcal{G}, \gamma)$ of agents so that $\gamma(B)$ is the quantity of agents in a measurable subset B of agents. The total quantity $\gamma(G)$ of agents is positive but need not be 1.

We suppose that the measure γ is atomless, meaning that there is an infinite number of agents none of which has a positive mass. The set of agents is therefore sometimes described as a "continuum." For example, agents could be uniformly distributed on the unit interval $G = [0, 1]$. Combining the continuum property with a notion of the independence of search across agents will lead in this chapter to an exact law of large numbers, by which the the cross-sectional distribution of search outcomes is deterministic (almost surely). For example, with two types of investors, *A* and *B*, we will see that independent random matching implies that the fraction of the population of type-*A* investors matched to type-*B* investors in a given period is almost surely equal to the probability that a given type-*A* investor is matched to some type-*B* investor.

Search delays are typical in OTC markets but also proxy for delays associated with reaching an awareness of trading opportunities, arranging financing and meeting suitable legal restrictions, negotiating trades, executing trades, and so on. As indicated in chapter 1 and theoretically modeled in chapters 4 and 5, these delays have important implications for optimal investment behavior, the dynamics of returns, and the distribution of information held across the population of investors.

3.2 RANDOM MATCHING

In the simplest and most common models of random matching, a typical agent α, whom we shall call Al, is randomly assigned to at most one other agent and not to himself. If Al is assigned to a particular agent β, whom we shall call Beth, then Beth is also assigned to Al. We suppose for now that the probability p of being matched to someone is the same for all agents and that the probability that an agent is matched to some agent in a particular measurable subset B of agents is proportional to the quantity $\gamma(B)$ of agents in that subset. This is a natural implementation of the idea that all agents are "equally likely" to be Al's counterparties. Thus, the probability that Al gets matched to someone in the set B must be $p\gamma(B)/\gamma(G)$.

In order to later rely on a law of large numbers for the independent random matching of agents, we assume a notion of joint measurability of match assignments, as functions on $\Omega \times G$, that is stated in appendix A. We will use the phrase "almost surely" to describe an event of probability 1, and use the phrase "for almost every agent" to describe a relationship that applies to every agent in G except those in some subset of measure 0.

We take the indicator random variable $1_{\alpha,\beta}$ to have the outcome 1 in the event that Al is matched to Beth, and 0 otherwise. By adding up, the indicator of the event that Al is matched to someone in a measurable set B of agents is the random variable

$$1_{\alpha,B} = \int_{\beta \in B} 1_{\alpha,\beta}\, d\gamma(\beta).$$

The quantity of matches of agents in A to agents in B is then

$$\int_{\alpha \in A} 1_{\alpha,B}\, d\gamma(\alpha).$$

By interchanging expectation and summation over agents (joint measurability justifies this application of Fubini's theorem), the expected quantity of these matches is

$$E\left[\int_{\alpha \in A} 1_{\alpha,B} d\gamma(\alpha)\right] = \int_{\alpha \in A} E(1_{\alpha,B})\, d\gamma(\alpha) = \gamma(A)p\frac{\gamma(B)}{\gamma(G)}. \tag{3.1}$$

Similarly, the expected quantity of matches of agents in B to agents in A is $p\gamma(B)\gamma(A)/\gamma(G)$. Thus, if A and B are disjoint, the total expected quantity of matches between agents in B and agents in A is $2p\gamma(B)\gamma(A)/\gamma(G)$.

For now, we suppose there is a finite number K of types of agents. For a two-type example, suppose that 60% of the agents are potential buyers of an asset and the remaining 40% are potential sellers. The total quantity $\gamma(G)$ of agents is, say, 10. Only buyer-to-seller or seller-to-buyer matches result in trades. Suppose that the probability p that a given agent is matched to someone is 0.5. From (3.1), the expected quantity of buyer-to-buyer matches is $0.5 \times 6 \times 0.6 = 1.8$, the expected quantity of seller-to-seller matches is $0.5 \times 4 \times 0.4 = 0.8$, and the expected quantity of buyer-to-seller matches is $0.5 \times 6 \times 0.4 = 1.2$, which is equal to the quantity of seller-to-buyer matches. Thus, the total expected quantity of matches is $1.8 + 2 \times 1.2 + 0.8 = 5$, which is indeed the same as the total quantity of agents multiplied by the 50% probability that any agent is matched.

By "independent random matching," we mean that, for almost every agent α, the matching result for α (the event of remaining unmatched or the agent to whom α is matched) is independent of the matching result for β, for almost every agent β. An implication of independent random matching is that, for almost every agent α, the type of agent to whom α is matched is independent of the type to whom another agent β is matched, for almost every other agent β. This independence property will allow us to apply the exact law of large numbers for random matching, stated in appendix A, to calculate the total quantity of matches of pairs of agents that are of given respective types.

The conventional law of large numbers is applied to a sequence X_1, $X_2, \ldots$ of independent random variables all with the same probability distribution ν. By this law, for any measurable subset B of outcomes of X_i, the empirical fraction

$$\nu_n(B) = \frac{1}{n} \sum_{j=1}^{n} 1_{\{X_j \in B\}} \tag{3.2}$$

of outcomes in B converges with increasing sample size n to $\mathbb{P}(X_i \in B)$ almost surely. That is, the empirical distribution ν_n converges (almost surely) to the underlying probability distribution ν.

The *exact* law of large numbers treats a family $\{X_\alpha : \alpha \in G\}$ of random variables, one for each agent, satisfying measurability conditions provided in appendix A. These random variables need not be identically distributed. We are interested in characterizing the cross-sectional empirical distribution μ of these random variables, defined at some subset B of outcomes as

$$\mu(B) = \frac{1}{\gamma(G)} \int_G 1_{\{X_\alpha \in B\}} \, d\gamma(\alpha),$$

the fraction of the outcomes that are in B, which is analogous to (3.2). Absent independence assumptions, this fraction $\mu(B)$ is a nontrivial random variable. Under the independence and technical conditions of the exact law of large numbers of Sun (2006) (theorem A.1 in appendix A), we have almost surely

$$\mu(B) = \frac{1}{\gamma(G)} \int_G \mathbb{P}(X_\alpha \in B) \, d\gamma(\alpha),$$

which is the cross-sectional average probability that X_α is in B. That is, with independence, the empirical distribution is almost surely the same as the average probability distribution.

When later modeling equilibrium investor behavior, our task is dramatically simplified if agents correctly assume that the empirical cross-sectional distribution of matches is not merely approximated by its probability distribution but is actually *equal* to it. This is known as the exact law of large

numbers for random matching, conditions for which are given by Duffie
and Sun (2007, 2011) and restated in appendix A. By this exact law, letting A_i denote the subset of type-i agents, the quantity of matches of type-
i agents to type-j agents is almost surely equal to the expected quantity,
$p\gamma(A_i)\gamma(A_j)/\gamma(G)$.

Thus, in our previous example, with independent random matching, the
quantity of buyer-to-seller matches is almost surely equal to the expected
quantity, $0.5 \times 6 \times 0.4 = 1.2$.

3.3 DYNAMIC SEARCH MODELS

In dynamic search models, random matching occurs period after period. In
many applications, when agents meet, the matching activity could change
the agents' types, perhaps randomly. For example, a prospective seller and a
prospective buyer could meet at random and, if they successfully negotiate
a trade, become a prospective buyer and a prospective seller, respectively.
This is the basis of the dynamics described in chapter 4. Through their bids
and offers agents could also exchange information with each other when
they meet, which changes their types with respect to posterior beliefs, as in
chapter 5. Agents' types could also change for exogenous reasons, such as
changes in preferences, exogenous investment opportunities, or new private
information.

For now we suppose that at integer times agents are randomly matched,
as in the previous section, and that the probabilities of matching assignments
and of exogenous type changes for each agent depend only on that agent's
current type and on the cross-sectional distribution of types in the population. As before, we assume independence of these events across almost every
pair of agents, as defined precisely in appendix A.

For a warm-up illustrative calculation, suppose that there are two types
of agents, buyers and sellers. Before entering the market in a given period, a
change in preferences (or endowments or trading constraints, for example)
could, at random, cause a buyer to become a seller with probability 0.4, and
a seller to become a buyer with probability 0.5. For almost every pair of
traders, these exogenous changes are assumed to be independent. The exact

law of large numbers implies that these exogenous changes, in the aggregate, cause 40% of the buyers to become sellers and 50% of the sellers to become buyers, almost surely.

An agent is randomly matched to another with probability 0.2. Whenever a buyer and a seller are matched, they leave the market. They otherwise stay.

The initial quantities of buyers and sellers are b and s, respectively. In each period, after mutation and matching, the quantity of new buyers entering the market is assumed to be 10% of the quantity of buyers in the previous period plus 4. The quantity of new sellers entering is 20% of the previous-period quantity of sellers plus 2. These entries occur after a trade. This example is contrived merely as an instructive numerical illustration.

An application of the exact law of large numbers implies that the new quantity of buyers is almost surely

$$b' = (0.6b + 0.5s) - 2 \times 0.2 \times (0.6b + 0.5s)\frac{0.4b + 0.5s}{b + s} + (0.1b + 4).$$

Similarly, the new quantity of sellers is almost surely

$$s' = (0.4b + 0.5s) - 2 \times 0.2 \times (0.4b + 0.5s)\frac{0.6b + 0.5s}{b + s} + (0.2s + 2).$$

The first-time reader should review each term in these expressions as a check on understanding.

One often simplifies with a "steady-state" model in which the quantities b and s of buyers and sellers are stationary, that is, $b' = b$ and $s' = s$. In order for this to be the case, the net quantity $Q_b = -0.4b + 0.5s + 0.1b + 4$ of additional new buyers arising from exogenous type changes and fresh arrivals must be equal to the quantity of buyer departures caused by trade. Because this is also the case for sellers and because the quantity of trades is of course the same for buyers and sellers, we have $Q_b = Q_s$. We therefore have the linear equation

$$-0.4b + 0.5s + 0.4b + 4 = 0.4b - 0.5s + 0.2s + 2,$$

which implies that

$$s = \frac{7}{8}b - \frac{5}{2}.$$

We can substitute this result for s into the steady-state equation

$$b = 0.6b + 0.5s - 2 \times 0.2 \times (0.6b + 0.5s)\frac{0.4b + 0.5s}{b + s} + 0.1b + 4$$

and arrive at the quadratic equation

$$\frac{359}{2500}b^2 - \frac{46}{5}b + 12 = 0,$$

whose unique positive real solution is $b \simeq 62.73$. We then find that $s \simeq 52.39$. If the market starts with these quantities of buyers and sellers, then these quantities will persist at all future times almost surely.

This notion of stationarity under dynamic random matching and mutation has been used for almost a century to model stability in population genetics, as discussed in section 3.8, which provides a brief outline of the development of the literature. This approach became popular in economics, mainly in order to simplify modeling or study the effect of independence, in the latter half of the twentieth century.

3.4   MARKOV CHAIN FOR TYPE

We now model the evolution of the cross-sectional distribution of agents' types as a dynamic system, letting μ_{it} denote the fraction of the population that is of type i at period t.

For simplicity, we take the total quantity $\gamma(G)$ of agents to be 1 and assume no entry or exit. Simplifying from the previous example, we assume that at each period, mutually exclusively, a given agent is (i) matched, (ii) mutates type, or (iii) is unaffected.

Each period, agents of type i are matched with probability p_i and are matched with equal likelihood to sets of agents of equal measure. Under this uniform-likelihood assumption, an agent of type i is therefore matched to an agent of type j with probability $p_i \mu_{jt}$. Immediately after such a match, we suppose that the type-i agent changes to type k with probability q_{ijk}. For instance, if agents are either owners ($i = 1$) or nonowners ($i = 2$) of an asset, and if nonowners and owners trade the asset whenever they meet (the nonowner becoming an owner, and vice versa), then $q_{122} = q_{211} = 1$ and all other q_{ijk} are 1 for $k = i$ and zero for $k \neq i$. The probability that a particular agent makes a one-period transition from type i to type k through matching is therefore $p_i \mu_{jt} q_{ijk}$.

A type-i agent becomes a type-k agent in the next period with an exogenous "mutation" probability Φ_{ik}. Thus, we have $p_i + \sum_k \Phi_{ik} = 1$. In order to apply the exact law of large numbers, we assume that these type changes are pairwise-independent, as stated precisely in definition 2 in appendix A. The parameters of the model are (p, q, Φ) and the initial cross-sectional type distribution μ_0.

By an inductive application of the exact law of large numbers (theorem A.3 in appendix A), the quantity of type-k agents satisfies (almost surely)

$$\mu_{k,t+1} = \sum_{i=1}^{K} \mu_{it} \left(\Phi_{ik} + p_i \sum_j \mu_{jt} q_{ijk} \right). \tag{3.3}$$

Letting $\mu_t = (\mu_{1t}, \ldots, \mu_{Kt})'$ denote the vector of fractions of each type of agent, we have (almost surely)

$$\mu_{t+1} = (\Phi + Q(p, q, \mu_t)) \mu_t, \tag{3.4}$$

where $Q(p, q, \mu_t)$ is the $K \times K$ matrix whose (i, k)-element is $p_i \sum_j \mu_{jt} q_{ijk}$. Details are given by Duffie and Sun (2011).

We can similarly model the probability transitions of a particular agent's type. For any particular agent, the probability π_{it} that this agent is of type i at time t satisfies, as a vector,

$$\pi_{t+1} = (\Phi + Q(p, q, \mu_t)) \pi_t. \tag{3.5}$$

This means that the agent's type is a Markov chain with deterministic but time-varying transition probabilities that depend on the current cross-sectional type distribution μ_t.

The transition matrices in (3.4) and (3.5) are the same. Thus, if the agent's initial type is drawn at random from the initial cross-sectional type distribution μ_0, it follows that $\pi_t = \mu_t$ for all t (almost surely). That is, the probability distribution of the given agent's type at any time t is identical to the deterministic cross-sectional distribution of types at that time.

From (3.4), a stationary vector μ_∞ of quantities of agents satisfies the algebraic Riccati (linear-quadratic polynomial) equation

$$0 = (\Phi - I + Q(p, q, \mu_\infty))\mu_\infty. \tag{3.6}$$

Duffie and Sun (2011) show that a stationary equilibrium exists. The same equation characterizes a stationary probability distribution π_∞ of a given agent's type.

3.5 CONTINUOUS-TIME SEARCH AND MATCHING

In many cases, calculations are simplified in a continuous-time setting. For this, we use the notion of an intensity process λ for the arrival of events of a particular type. The intensity λ_t of a given event is defined as the conditional mean arrival rate of the event given all of the information available up until time t. For example, an intensity of 2 means an expected arrival rate of two events per unit of time. The mathematical foundations are reviewed in appendix B. A special case is a constant intensity λ, the Poisson-process model by which the times between arrivals are independent and exponentially distributed with mean $1/\lambda$.

Now, suppose that an agent of type i is randomly matched to other agents at a constant intensity λ_i. Taking our typical assumption that the selection of a counterparty is uniform across the population, the intensity of matches to agents of type j is $\lambda_i \mu_{jt}$. When such a match occurs, we suppose that the agent of type i becomes an agent of type k with probability q_{ijk}, as in the discrete-time model in the previous section. The type of an agent can also mutate from i to k for other reasons, at a fixed intensity of η_{ik}. For example, chapter 4 discusses mutation over time of an investor's preferences for the asset or the investor's liquidity needs.

Assuming, for almost every pair of agents, that these type transitions are independent and that the exact law of large numbers applies, the quantity μ_{kt} of type-k agents satisfies (almost surely) the ordinary differential equation

$$\frac{d}{dt}\mu_{kt} = \sum_i \eta_{ik}\mu_{it} - \lambda_k \mu_{kt} + \sum_i \sum_j \lambda_i \mu_{it} \mu_{jt} q_{ijk}, \tag{3.7}$$

where we define $\eta_{kk} = -1$ to capture the expected rate of change of mutation out of type k. The dynamic equation for $\mu_t = (\mu_{1t}, \ldots, \mu_{Kt})'$ is thus

$$\frac{d}{dt}\mu_t = (\eta + Q(\lambda, q, \mu_t))\mu_t \tag{3.8}$$

for the same matrix-valued function $Q(\cdot)$ defined in the previous section. As of this writing, a rigorous justification of (3.8) based on independent random matching has yet to be provided.[1] In particle physics, Boltzmann referred to this form of application by assumption of the continuous-time exact law of large numbers for random matching as the *Stosszahlansatz*. We will proceed as though this ansatz applies. Ferland and Giroux (2008) and Reminik (2009) have shown in some settings that the type distributions of discrete-time or finite-agent models converge to the solution of (3.8) as the number of agents converges to infinity and the length of a time period converges to zero.

The algebraic Riccati equation corresponding to the stationary quantities of each type is

$$0 = (\eta + Q(\lambda, q, \mu_\infty))\mu_\infty, \tag{3.9}$$

which is identical to the discrete-time equation (3.6) after replacing $\Phi - I$ and p with their continuous-time counterparts η and λ, respectively. The discrete-time model, however, was restricted by assuming that at each time period the events of being matched and of having an exogenous type change are mutually exclusive. Without such a restriction, the discrete-time model would be slightly more complicated than the corresponding continuous-time model.

3.6   OPTIMAL SEARCH

Continuing in this continuous-time framework, suppose that an agent of type i collects utility at the rate $u(i)$ whenever of type i and generates an additional utility (or expected utility) of $w(i,j)$ when matched to an agent of type j. The dynamics of type changes are determined by the meeting intensities of agents and by the parameters η and q_{ijk} whose roles were explained in the

---

[1] This is a subject of current research by the author and Yeneng Sun.

previous section. As opposed to the previous section, however, each agent chooses some search intensity process λ. Search with intensity process λ generates costs at the rate $c(\lambda_t)$ at time t, for some continuous $c:[0,\infty) \to \mathbb{R}$. The search intensity process is bounded above by some constant $\overline{\lambda}$. The agent's search intensity process λ must be based only on information that the agent has available. More precisely, the intensity process is assumed to be predictable with respect to the agent's information filtration, as defined in appendix B.

To simplify, suppose that the agent conjectures that the population cross-sectional type distribution μ is constant. The agent's type process associated with a chosen intensity process λ is denoted ϕ^λ.

For a discount rate $r > 0$, the agent's lifetime expected discounted utility is then

$$U(\lambda) = E\left(\int_0^\infty e^{-rt}[u(\phi_t^\lambda) - c(\lambda_t)]dt + \sum_{k=1}^\infty e^{-rT_k} w(\phi^\lambda(T_k-),\theta_k) \right),$$

where T_k is the time of the kth match of that agent to some other agent, $\phi^\lambda(T_k-)$ is the type of the agent immediately before any type change occurs at time T_k, and θ_k is the type to whom the agent is matched at time T_k.

We are interested in solving the stochastic control problem

$$\sup_\lambda U(\lambda). \tag{3.10}$$

A search intensity process λ^* is optimal if it solves this problem, that is, if $U(\lambda^*) \geq U(\lambda)$ for all λ.

Letting $V = (V(1), \ldots, V(K))$ denote the supremum utilities associated with the respective types, the Hamilton-Jacobi-Bellman (HJB) equation for optimal choice of intensity is

$$0 = \sup_{\ell \in [0,\overline{\lambda}]} B(i,V,\ell), \quad i \in \{1,\ldots,K\}, \tag{3.11}$$

where

$$B(i,V,\ell) = -rV(i) + u(i) - c(\ell) + \sum_{k=1}^K \eta_{ik}(V(k) - V(i))$$
$$+ \ell \sum_{j=1}^K \mu_j \left[w(i,j) + \sum_{k=1}^K q_{ijk}(V(k) - V(i)) \right].$$

There is a unique V solving the HJB equation (3.11). Fixing a solution V of the HJB equation, the continuity of $B(i, V, \ell)$ with respect to ℓ implies that the supremum defined by (3.11) is attained by some intensity level denoted by $\Lambda(i)$. We conjecture that optimality is achieved by an intensity process that has the outcome $\Lambda(i)$ whenever the agent is of type i. We let ϕ^* denote a type process for the agent with this property. The corresponding search intensity process λ^* is then defined by $\lambda_t^* = \Lambda(\phi_{t-}^*)$. We thus conjecture that λ^* solves (3.10).

Proposition 3.1 *Problem (3.10) is solved by the search intensity process λ^*.*

This result follows from a standard verification argument, as follows. For an arbitrary search intensity process λ, let ϕ^λ be the associated type process and let

$$Y_t = e^{-rt} V(\phi_t^\lambda) + \int_0^t e^{-rs}[u(\phi_s^\lambda) - c(\lambda_s)]\, ds + \sum_{\{k:T_k \leq t\}} e^{-rT_k} w(\phi_{T_k-}^\lambda, \theta_k).$$

A calculation shows that a martingale Z is defined by

$$Z_t = Y_t - \int_0^t e^{-rs} B(\phi_s^\lambda, V(\phi_s^\lambda), \lambda_s)\, ds. \tag{3.12}$$

To check that Z is indeed a martingale, we let N_t be the number of type changes the agent has experienced by time t. Proposition B.2 implies that a martingale $\hat{N}$ is defined by

$$\hat{N}_t = N_t - \int_0^t \left[\eta_{\phi_s^\lambda, k} + \lambda_s \sum_j \mu_j\, q_{\phi_s^\lambda, j, k} \right] ds.$$

The fact that Z is a martingale now follows from another application of proposition B.2 and the fact that

$$dZ_t = dY_t - e^{-rt} B(\phi_t^\lambda, V(\phi_t^\lambda), \lambda_t)\, dt = H_t\, d\hat{N}_t,$$

where H is a bounded process that can be calculated.

From the HJB equation, $B(\phi_s^\lambda, V(\phi_s^\lambda), \lambda_s) \leq 0$, so Y is a supermartingale. Thus, for an agent of initial type i and for any time t,

$$V(i) = Y_0 \geq E(Y_t).$$

Because $e^{-rt}\max_i |V(i)|$ converges with t to zero, $E(Y_t) \to U(\lambda)$, and we have

$$V(\phi_0^\lambda) \geq U(\lambda).$$

For the particular case of $\lambda = \lambda^*$, the HJB equation (3.11) implies that $B(\phi_s^*, V(\phi_s^*), \lambda_s^*) = 0$, so Y is a martingale, and again taking a limit,

$$V(\phi_0^*) = U(\lambda^*).$$

Because $\phi_0^* = \phi_0^\lambda$ is an arbitrary initial type, $U(\lambda^*) \geq U(\lambda)$, proving optimality of λ^*, and confirming that $V(i)$ is the optimal utility $U(\lambda^*)$ of an agent of initial type i.

3.7   EQUILIBRIUM SEARCH INTENSITIES

Continuing in the setting of the previous section, an equilibrium is a cross-sectional distribution μ of types with the property that, when μ is taken as given by each agent, the optimal search intensities of agents are in aggregate consistent with μ. In order to formulate this precisely, suppose that for each cross-sectional type distribution μ, the dependence of an optimal search intensity policy function $\Lambda(\cdot)$, characterized in the last section, on the assumed cross-sectional distribution μ is indicated by writing $\Lambda^\mu = \Lambda$.

So, an equilibrium can be viewed as a solution μ (in the set Δ^{K-1} of nonnegative vectors in $\mathbb{R}^K$ that sum to 1) of the equilibrium equation

$$0 = (\eta + Q(\Lambda^\mu, q, \mu))\mu. \tag{3.13}$$

It would be enough for the existence of an equilibrium to have continuity of the map from a conjectured distribution $\nu \in \Delta^{K-1}$ to the corresponding solution μ of the stationary-measure equation

$$0 = (\eta + Q(\Lambda^\nu, q, \nu))\mu. \tag{3.14}$$

Because Δ^{K-1} is compact and convex, Schauder's theorem would then imply at least one equilibrium.

The purpose of this section is merely to explain the notion of equilibrium search intensities. We do not apply this notion here. An example is the model of equilibrium search intensities of Duffie, Malamud, and Manso (2009).

Our reliance on the exact law of large numbers for random matching is evident in the formulation of an agent's conjectures about the equilibrium market environment. In the proposed equilibrium, the agent correctly conjectures a deterministic distribution μ of types in the population. If μ is only a limiting approximation of the distribution of types as the number of agents gets larger and larger, then it could be substantially more difficult to characterize the agent's optimal search policy in a particular finite-agent setting. Moreover, it would not be assured that as the actual cross-sectional distribution of types converges to the limit distribution μ, the agent's optimal policy converges to the optimal policy associated with the limit distribution. For both of these reasons, the exact law of large numbers drastically simplifies our modeling. This tractability, however, is achieved at a cost in realism. Real market environments are much more complicated than our simple model suggests.

3.8   DEVELOPMENT OF THE SEARCH LITERATURE

Historically,[2] reliance on the exact law of large numbers for independent random matching dates back at least to 1908, when G.H. Hardy and W. Weinberg[3] independently proposed that random mating over time in a large population leads to constant and easily calculated fractions of each allele in the population. Hardy wrote: "Suppose that the numbers are fairly large, so that the mating may be regarded as random," and then used, in effect, an exact law of large numbers for random matching to deduce his results. Consider, for illustration, a continuum population of gametes consisting of two alleles, A and B, in initial proportions p and $q = 1 - p$. Then, following the Hardy-Weinberg approach, the new population would have a fraction p^2 whose parents are both of type A, a fraction q^2 whose parents are both of type B, and a fraction $2pq$ whose parents are of mixed type (heterozygotes). These genotypic proportions asserted by Hardy and Weinberg are already implicitly based on the exact law of large numbers for independent random matching in a large population.

---

[2] These historical remarks are based in part on Duffie and Sun (2007).
[3] See Hardy (1908) and Cavalli-Sforza and Bodmer (1971).

In the field of economics, Hellwig (1976) was the first, to my knowledge, to have relied on the effect of the exact law of large numbers for random pairwise matching in a market, in a 1976 study of a monetary exchange economy. (Diamond (1971) had earlier assumed random matching of a large population with finitely many employers but not pairwise matching among a continuum of agents.)

Since the 1970s, a large economics literature has routinely relied on an exact law of large numbers for independent random matching in a continuum population. This implicit use of this result occurs in general equilibrium theory (e.g., Gale (1986a, 1986b), McLennan and Sonnenschein (1991), Wolinsky (1990)), game theory (for example, Binmore and Samuelson (1999), Burdzy, Frankel, and Pauzner (2001), Dekel and Scotchmer (1999), Fudenberg and Levine (1993), Harrington (1998), monetary theory (for example, Diamond and Yellin (1990), Green and Zhou (2002), Hellwing (1976), Kiyotaki and Wright (1993)), labor economics (for example, Diamond (1982), Hosios (1990), Mortensen (1982), Mortensen and Pissarides (1994)), and financial market theory (for example, Duffie, Gârleanu, and Pedersen (2007), Krainer and LeRoy (2002)).

In almost all of this literature, dynamics are crucial. For example, in the monetary and finance literature cited above, each agent in the economy solves a dynamic programming problem based on the conjectured dynamics of the cross-sectional distribution of agent types. An equilibrium has the property that the combined effect of individually optimal dynamic behavior is consistent with the conjectured population dynamics. In order to simplify the analysis, much of the literature relies on equilibria with a stationary distribution of agent types, as in the previous section.

CHAPTER 4

A Simple OTC Pricing Model

This chapter, based entirely on Duffie, Gârleanu, and Pedersen (2005, 2007),[1] presents a simple introduction to asset pricing in OTC markets. Investors search for opportunities to trade and bargain with counterparties, each counterparty being aware that failure to conduct a trade could lead to a costly new search for a counterparty. In equilibrium, whenever there is gain from trade, the opportunity to search for a new counterparty is dominated by trading at the equilibrium asset price. The asset price reflects the degree of search frictions.

Under conditions, illiquidity premia are higher when counterparties are harder to find, when sellers have less bargaining power, when the fraction of qualified owners is smaller, and when risk aversion, volatility, or hedging demand is larger. Supply shocks cause prices to jump, and then "recover" over time, with a pattern that depends on the degree of search frictions.

We show how the equilibrium bargaining powers of the counterparties are determined by search opportunities using the approach of Rubinstein and Wolinsky (1985).

Here, traders have the same information. The case of OTC trading with asymmetric information is treated in chapter 5.

4.1 BASIC RISK-NEUTRAL OTC PRICING MODEL

This section introduces a simple model of asset pricing in an OTC market with risk-neutral investors. Later, we incorporate the effects of risk aversion.

---

[1] Material in this chapter is adapted from Darrell Duffie, Nicolae Gârleanu, and Lasse Heje Pedersen, "Valuation in Over-the-Counter Markets," *Review of Financial Studies* 20 (2007), 1865–1900, published by Oxford University Press.

We fix a nonatomic measure space of investors. Each is infinitely lived, with a constant time-preference rate $\beta > 0$ for consumption of a single non-storable numéraire good. A probability space and a common information filtration are also fixed. A cumulative consumption process C is one that can be represented as the difference between an increasing adapted process and a decreasing adapted process, with C_t denoting the total amount of consumption that has occurred through time t. The agent is restricted to a consumption process C whose utility

$$U(C) = E\left(\int_0^\infty e^{-\beta t} \, dC_t\right)$$

is well defined. This allows for positive or negative consumption "smoothly" over time or in sudden "lumps."

An agent can invest at any time in a liquid security with a risk-free interest rate of r. As a natural form of credit constraint, the agent must enforce some lower bound on the liquid wealth process W. (Otherwise, the agent could borrow without limit and get unbounded utility.) We take $r = \beta$ in this baseline model.

Agents may trade a long-lived asset in an OTC market in which trade may be negotiated bilaterally whenever two counterparties are matched. For simplicity, we begin by taking the traded asset to be a consol, a bond that continually pays one unit of consumption per unit of time. We later allow random dividend processes in order to examine the effects of risk aversion.

An agent has an intrinsic preference for asset ownership that is high or low. A low-type agent, when owning the asset, has an asset holding cost of δ per time unit. A high-type agent has no such holding cost. We could imagine this holding cost to be a shadow price for ownership due, for example, to a pressing need for cash or a relatively low personal use for the asset, as may happen for certain durable consumption goods. When we later allow for risk aversion, the low-type agent will be one whose endowments are adversely correlated with the asset dividends.

The agent's intrinsic type is a Markov chain, switching from low to high with intensity λ_u and back to low with intensity λ_d. The intrinsic-type processes of almost every pair of agents are independent. These occasional preference shocks will generate incentives to trade because in equilibrium low-type owners want to sell and high-type nonowners want to buy.

The per-capita supply s of the asset is initially endowed to a subset of the agents. As a simplification, investors can hold at most one unit of the asset and cannot shortsell. This restriction is relaxed by Gârleanu (2009) and by Lagos and Rocheteau (2009). Because agents have linear utility, it is without much loss of generality that we restrict attention to equilibria in which, at any given time and state of the world, an agent holds either 0 or 1 unit of the asset. The set of $K = 4$ agent types is then $\mathcal{T} = \{ho, hn, lo, ln\}$, with the letters h and l designating the agent's current intrinsic preference state as high or low, respectively, and with o or n indicating whether the agent currently owns the asset or not, respectively.

We adopt the continuous-time search and bargaining framework of Trejos and Wright (1995). We let $\mu_\sigma(t)$ denote the fraction at time t of agents of type $\sigma \in \mathcal{T}$, so that

$$1 = \mu_{ho}(t) + \mu_{hn}(t) + \mu_{lo}(t) + \mu_{ln}(t). \tag{4.1}$$

Equating the per-capita supply s with the fraction of owners gives

$$s = \mu_{ho}(t) + \mu_{lo}(t). \tag{4.2}$$

Any agent is matched to some counterparty with a constant intensity of λ, a parameter reflecting the efficiency of the market technology and perhaps also reflecting individual inattention to trading. We assume that the counterparty found is randomly selected from the pool of other agents, so that the probability that the counterparty is of type σ is $\mu_\sigma(t)$. Thus, the total intensity of being matched to a type-σ investor at time t is $\lambda \mu_\sigma(t)$. Based on the *Stosszahlansatz* outlined in chapter 3, hn investors thus meet lo investors at an aggregate (almost sure) rate of $\lambda \mu_{lo}(t) \mu_{hn}(t)$.

In keeping with the modeling convention used in other chapters, we are departing here from the notion of contact intensity of Duffie, Gârleanu, and Pedersen (2005, 2007), which measures the intensity with which an agent contacts other agents (in a transitive-verb sense) separately from the intensity with which other agents contact the agent in question. The total intensity of being matched is the sum of these two. Thus, the intensity parameter used by Duffie, Gârlcanu, and Pedersen (2005, 2007) is half of that used here.

To solve the model, we proceed in two steps. First, we exploit the fact that the only form of encounter that provides gains from trade is one in which low-type owners meet high-type nonowners.

In any equilibrium of the bargaining game played at each such encounter, trade occurs immediately. We can therefore determine the asset allocations without reference to prices. Given the time dynamics of the cross-sectional type distribution $\mu(t)$, we then consider equilibrium asset pricing.

In equilibrium, the rates of change of the fractions of the respective investor types satisfy the special case of (3.8) given by

$$
\begin{aligned}
\dot{\mu}_{lo}(t) &= -\lambda \mu_{hn}(t)\mu_{lo}(t) - \lambda_u \mu_{lo}(t) + \lambda_d \mu_{ho}(t), \\
\dot{\mu}_{hn}(t) &= -\lambda \mu_{hn}(t)\mu_{lo}(t) - \lambda_d \mu_{hn}(t) + \lambda_u \mu_{ln}(t), \\
\dot{\mu}_{ho}(t) &= \lambda \mu_{hn}(t)\mu_{lo}(t) - \lambda_d \mu_{ho}(t) + \lambda_u \mu_{lo}(t), \\
\dot{\mu}_{ln}(t) &= \lambda \mu_{hn}(t)\mu_{lo}(t) - \lambda_u \mu_{ln}(t) + \lambda_d \mu_{hn}(t),
\end{aligned}
\tag{4.3}
$$

where $\dot{\mu}(t)$ denotes the time derivative of $\mu(t)$.

The intuition for, say, the first equation in (4.3) is straightforward: Whenever an *lo* agent meets an *hn* investor, he sells his asset and is no longer an *lo* agent. This explains the first term on the right-hand side of (4.3). The second term is due to intrinsic type changes in which *lo* investors become *ho* investors, and the last term is due to intrinsic type changes from *ho* to *lo*.

Duffie, Gârleanu, and Pedersen (2005) show that there is a unique stable stationary solution for $\{\mu(t): t \geq 0\}$, that is, a constant solution defined by $\dot{\mu}(t)=0$. The steady state is computed by using (4.1) and (4.2) and the fact that $\mu_{lo} + \mu_{ln} = \lambda_d/(\lambda_u + \lambda_d)$ in order to write the first equation in (4.3) as a quadratic equation in μ_{lo}.

Having determined the stationary fractions of investor types, we compute the investors' equilibrium intensities of finding counterparties of each type and hence their utilities for remaining lifetime consumption, as well as the bargained price P. The utility of a particular agent depends on the agent's current type $\sigma(t) \in \mathcal{T}$ and the wealth W_t held in the liquid "bank-account" asset. Specifically, an agent's continuation utility is $W_t + V_{\sigma(t)}$, where, for each investor type σ in $\mathcal{T}$, V_σ is a constant to be determined.

In steady state, the Bellman principle implies that the rate of growth of any agent's expected indirect utility must be the discount rate r, which yields the steady-state equations

$$0 = rV_{lo} - \lambda_u(V_{ho} - V_{lo}) - \lambda\mu_{hn}(P - V_{lo} + V_{ln}) - (1 - \delta),$$
$$0 = rV_{ln} - \lambda_u(V_{hn} - V_{ln}),$$
$$0 = rV_{ho} + \lambda_d(V_{ho} - V_{lo}) - 1,$$
$$0 = rV_{hn} + \lambda_d(V_{hn} - V_{ln}) - \lambda\mu_{lo}(V_{ho} - V_{hn} - P).$$

$$(4.4)$$

4.2 BARGAINING OVER THE PRICE

The asset price is determined through bilateral bargaining. A high-type non-owner pays at most his reservation value $\Delta V_h = V_{ho} - V_{hn}$ for obtaining the asset, while a low-type owner requires a price of at least $\Delta V_l = V_{lo} - V_{ln}$. In any equilibrium of the bargaining game, trade must occur at an in-between price of the form

$$P = \Delta V_l(1 - q) + \Delta V_h q \tag{4.5}$$

where $q \in [0, 1]$ is called the "bargaining power" of the seller. Because we are characterizing stationary equilibrium, we take the bargaining power q to be constant.

While a Nash equilibrium in the bargaining game is consistent with any exogenously assumed bargaining power, we can use the device of Rubinstein and Wolinsky (1985) to calculate the unique bargaining power that represents the limiting price of a sequence of economies in which, once a pair of counterparties meets to negotiate, one of the pair is selected at random to make an offer to the other at each of a sequence of offer times separated by intervals that shrink to zero.

Specifically, suppose that when an owner who wishes to sell and a non-owner who wishes to buy find each other, one of them is chosen randomly, the seller with probability $\hat{q}$ and the buyer with probability $1 - \hat{q}$, to suggest a trading price. The counterparty either rejects or accepts the offer immediately. If the offer is rejected, the owner receives the dividend from the asset during the current period. At the next period, T later, one of the two agents is chosen independently at random to make a new offer. The bargaining may, however, break down before a counteroffer is made. A breakdown may occur because, during the interim, at least one of the agents may change his or her intrinsic valuation type or one of the agents may meet yet another agent and leave his or her current trading partner. (The opportunity to continue to search for alternative counterparties while engaged in negotiation will also be considered below.)

This bargaining setting is a slight extension of our basic model in that, once a pair of agents meet, they are given the opportunity to interact at discretely separated moments in time, T apart. Later, we return to our original continuous-time framework by letting T go to zero and adopt the limiting behavior of their bargaining game as $T \to 0$.

We consider first the case in which agents can search for alternative counterparties during their bargaining encounter. We assume that, given contact with an alternative partner, they leave the present partner in order to negotiate with the newly found one. The offerer suggests the price that leaves the other agent indifferent between accepting and rejecting it. In the unique subgame perfect equilibrium, the offer is accepted immediately, as shown by Rubinstein (1982). The value of rejecting is that associated with the assumption by agents that the equilibrium strategies are to be played from then onward. Letting P_σ be the price suggested by the agent of type $\sigma \in \{lo, hn\}$, letting $\bar{P} = \hat{q}P_{lo} + (1 - \hat{q})P_{hn}$, and making use of the dynamic equations governing V_{lo} and V_{hn}, we have

$$P_{hn} - \Delta V_l = e^{-(r + \lambda_d + \lambda_u + \lambda\mu_{lo} + \lambda\mu_{hn})T}(\bar{P} - \Delta V_l) + O(T^2), \qquad (4.6)$$
$$-P_{lo} + \Delta V_h = e^{-(r + \lambda_d + \lambda_u + \lambda\mu_{lo} + \lambda\mu_{hn})T}(-\bar{P} + \Delta V_h) + O(T^2). \qquad (4.7)$$

These prices, P_{hn} and P_{lo}, have the same limit $P = \lim_{T \to 0} P_{hn} = \lim_{T \to 0} P_{lo}$. The limit price P and a limit type-dependent value V_σ satisfy

$$P = \Delta V_l(1 - q) + \Delta V_h q, \qquad (4.8)$$

with

$$q = \hat{q}. \qquad (4.9)$$

Thus, the limiting bargaining power $q = \hat{q}$ does not depend on the model parameters beyond the likelihood that the seller is chosen to make an offer. In particular, an agent's intensity of meeting other trading partners does not influence q. This is because one's own ability to meet an alternative trading partner makes one more impatient and also increases the partner's risk of breakdown. These two effects happen to cancel each other.

Other bargaining procedures lead to other outcomes. For instance, if agents are unable to search for alternative trading partners during negotiation, then, as shown by Duffie, Gârleanu, and Pedersen (2005),

$$q = \frac{\hat{q}(r + \lambda_u + \lambda_d + \lambda\mu_{lo})}{\hat{q}(r + \lambda_u + \lambda_d + \lambda\mu_{lo}) + (1 - \hat{q})(r + \lambda_u + \lambda_d + \lambda\mu_{hn})}. \tag{4.10}$$

The linear system of equations defined by (4.4) and (4.5) has a unique solution, with

$$P = \frac{1}{r} - \frac{\delta}{r} \frac{r(1 - q) + \lambda_d + \lambda\mu_{lo}(1 - q)}{r + \lambda_d + \lambda\mu_{lo}(1 - q) + \lambda_u + \lambda\mu_{hn}q}. \tag{4.11}$$

This price (4.11) is the present value $1/r$ of dividends reduced by an illiquidity discount. The discount is larger (other effects held constant) if the distressed owner has less hope of switching type (lower λ_u), if the quantity μ_{hn} of other buyers to be found is smaller, if the buyer may more suddenly need liquidity himself (higher λ_d), if it is easier for the buyer to find other sellers (higher μ_{lo}), or if the seller has less bargaining power (lower q).

These intuitive results are based on partial derivatives of the right-hand side of (4.11). In other words, they hold when a parameter changes without influencing any of the others. It is the case, however, that the steady-state-type fractions μ themselves depend on λ_d, λ_u, and λ, an equilibrium effect that must also be considered. The following proposition offers a characterization of the equilibrium steady-state effect of changing each parameter.

Proposition 4.1 *The steady-state equilibrium price P is decreasing in δ, s, and λ_d and is increasing in λ_u and q. Further, if $s < \lambda_u/(\lambda_u + \lambda_d)$, then $P \to 1/r$ as $\lambda \to \infty$ and P is increasing in λ for all $\lambda \geq \bar{\lambda}$ for a constant $\bar{\lambda}$ depending on the other parameters of the model.*

The condition that $s < \lambda_u/(\lambda_u + \lambda_d)$ means that, in steady state, there is less than one unit of asset per agent of high intrinsic type. Under this condition, the Walrasian frictionless price is equal to the present value of dividends $1/r$ because the marginal owner is always a high-type agent who incurs no holding costs. Naturally, as the search intensity increases toward infinity and frictions vanish, the OTC price approaches the Walrasian price (that is, the liquidity discount vanishes). The proposition also states that the price decreases with the ratio s of assets to qualified owners, with reductions in the mean arrival rate λ_d of a liquidity shock and with increases in the speed at which agents can "recover" by becoming of high type again. It can easily be seen that if agents can easily recover (that is, as $\lambda_u \to \infty$), the price also approaches the Walrasian price.

While the proposition above captures the intuitively anticipated increase in market value with increasing search intensity λ, the alternative is also possible. With $s > \lambda_u/(\lambda_u + \lambda_d)$, the marginal investor in perfect markets has the relatively lower reservation value and search frictions lead to a "scarcity value." For example, a high-type investor in an illiquid OTC market could pay more than the Walrasian price for the asset because it is hard to find, and given no opportunity to exploit the effect of immediate competition among many sellers. This scarcity value could, for example, contribute to the widely studied on-the-run premium for Treasuries or to the elevation of prices of bonds that are difficult to find for physical settlement of credit derivatives or futures contracts. Absent search delays, it is difficult to explain these pricing phenomena.

4.3   RISK AVERSION

We turn to a close variant of the basic asset-pricing model that allows risk aversion. The motive for trade between two agents is the different extents to which they can use the asset to hedge their endowment risks. We will show that with "small" hedging motives, this economy behaves like the baseline risk-neutral model, with hedging motives approximated by the holding cost parameter δ.

Agents have constant absolute-risk-averse (CARA) additive utility, with a coefficient γ of absolute risk aversion and with time preference at rate β. An asset has a cumulative dividend process D satisfying

$$dD_t = m_D \, dt + \sigma_D \, dB_t,$$

where m_D and σ_D are constants and B is a standard Brownian motion with respect to the given probability space and information filtration. Agent i has a cumulative endowment process η^i, with

$$d\eta^i_t = m_\eta \, dt + \sigma_\eta \, dB^i_t,$$

where the standard Brownian motion B^i is defined by

$$dB^i_t = \rho^i_t \, dB_t + \sqrt{1 - (\rho^i_t)^2} \, dZ^i_t$$

for a standard Brownian motion Z^i independent of B. Thus, ρ^i_t can be viewed as the "instantaneous correlation" between the asset dividend and the endowment of agent i. The correlation process ρ^i is a two-state Markov chain with states ρ_h and $\rho_l > \rho_h$. The intrinsic type of an agent is identified with this correlation parameter. An agent i whose intrinsic type is currently high (that is, with $\rho^i_t = \rho_h$) values the asset more highly than does a low-intrinsic-type agent because of relative hedging preferences, that is, because the increments of the high-type endowment have lower (more favorable) conditional correlation with the asset's dividends.

As in the baseline model in section 4.1, agents' intrinsic types are pairwise-independent Markov chains, switching from l to h with intensity λ_u and from h to l with intensity λ_d. An agent owns either θ_n or θ_o units of the asset, where $\theta_n < \theta_o$. For simplicity, no other positions are permitted, which entails a loss in generality. The agent type space is $\mathcal{T} = \{lo, ln, ho, hn\}$, where the symbols o and n now indicate large and small owners, respectively.

Given a total supply Θ of shares per investor, market clearing requires that

$$(\mu_{lo} + \mu_{ho})\theta_o + (\mu_{ln} + \mu_{hn})\theta_n = \Theta,$$

which, using (4.1), implies that the fraction of large owners is

$$\mu_{lo} + \mu_{ho} = s \equiv \frac{\Theta - \theta_n}{\theta_o - \theta_n}. \tag{4.12}$$

We consider a particular agent whose type process is $\{\sigma(t) : t \geq 0\}$ and let θ denote the associated asset-position process; that is, $\theta(t) = \theta_o$ whenever $\sigma(t) \in \{ho, lo\}$ and otherwise $\theta(t) = \theta_n$. We suppose that there is a perfectly liquid "money-market" asset with a constant risk-free rate of return r, which, for simplicity, is fixed exogenously. This liquid asset has a perfectly elastic supply, as is typical in the literature, such as Wang (1994), that treats multi-period asset-pricing models based on CARA utility.

The agent's money-market wealth process W therefore satisfies

$$dW_t = (rW_t - c_t)\, dt + \theta_t\, dD_t + d\eta_t - P\, d\theta_t,$$

where c is the agent's consumption process, η is the agent's cumulative endowment process, and P is the asset price per share (which is constant in the equilibria that we examine in this section). The last term thus captures payments in connection with trade. The consumption process c is required to be jointly measurable in time and state of the world, adapted to the information filtration, and bounded.

We consider a steady-state equilibrium and let $J(w, \sigma)$ denote the indirect utility of an agent of type $\sigma \in \{lo, ln, ho, hn\}$ with current wealth w. Assuming sufficient differentiability, the HJB equation for an agent of current type lo is

$$
\begin{aligned}
0 = \sup_{\bar{c} \in \mathbb{R}} \{ &-e^{-\gamma \bar{c}} + J_w(w, lo)(rw - \bar{c} + \theta_o m_D + m_\eta) \\
&+ \tfrac{1}{2} J_{ww}(w, lo)(\theta_o^2 \sigma_D^2 + \sigma_\eta^2 + 2\rho_t \theta_o \sigma_D \sigma_\eta) - \beta J(w, lo) \\
&+ \lambda_u [J(w, ho) - J(w, lo)] + \lambda \mu_{hn}[J(w + P\bar{\theta}, ln) - J(w, lo)] \},
\end{aligned}
$$

where $\bar{\theta} = \theta_o - \theta_n$. The HJB equations of the other agent types are analogous. Under technical regularity conditions stated in Duffie, Gârleanu, and Pedersen (2007),

$$J(w, \sigma) = -e^{-r\gamma(w + a_\sigma + \bar{a})}, \tag{4.13}$$

where

$$\bar{a} = \frac{1}{r}\left(\frac{\log r}{\gamma} + m_\eta - \frac{1}{2} r\gamma \sigma_\eta^2 - \frac{r - \beta}{r\gamma} \right),$$

and where, for each type σ, the constant a_σ is determined as follows. The first-order conditions of the HJB equation of an agent of type σ imply an optimal consumption rate of

$$-\frac{\log(r)}{\gamma} + r(w + a_\sigma + \bar{a}). \tag{4.14}$$

Inserting this consumption rate into the respective HJB equations yields a system of equations characterizing the coefficients $\{a_\sigma : \sigma \in \mathcal{T}\}$.

The price P is determined using Nash bargaining with seller bargaining power q, as in the baseline model in section 4.1. Given the reservation values of buyer and seller implied by $J(w, \sigma)$, the bargaining price satisfies $a_{lo} - a_{ln} \le P\bar{\theta} \le a_{ho} - a_{hn}$.

Proposition 4.2 *In equilibrium, an agent of type σ with wealth w consumes at the rate (4.14) and has the value function given by (4.13), where $(a_{lo}, a_{ln}, a_{ho}, a_{hn}, P) \in \mathbb{R}^5$ solve*

$$
\begin{aligned}
0 &= ra_{lo} + \lambda_u \frac{e^{-r\gamma(a_{ho} - a_{lo})} - 1}{r\gamma} + \lambda\mu_{hn} \frac{e^{-r\gamma(P\bar{\theta} + a_{ln} - a_{lo})} - 1}{r\gamma} - (\kappa(\theta_o) - \theta_o\bar{\delta}), \\
0 &= ra_{ln} + \lambda_u \frac{e^{-r\gamma(a_{hn} - a_{ln})} - 1}{r\gamma} - (\kappa(\theta_n) - \theta_n\bar{\delta}), \\
0 &= ra_{ho} + \lambda_d \frac{e^{-r\gamma(a_{lo} - a_{ho})} - 1}{r\gamma} - \kappa(\theta_o), \\
0 &= ra_{hn} + \lambda_d \frac{e^{-r\gamma(a_{ln} - a_{hn})} - 1}{r\gamma} + \lambda\mu_{lo} \frac{e^{-r\gamma(-P\bar{\theta} + a_{ho} - a_{hn})} - 1}{r\gamma} - \kappa(\theta_n),
\end{aligned}
\tag{4.15}
$$

and

$$
q\left(1 - e^{r\gamma(P\bar{\theta} - (a_{lo} - a_{ln}))}\right) = (1 - q)\left(1 - e^{r\gamma(-P\bar{\theta} + a_{ho} - a_{hn})}\right),
\tag{4.16}
$$

where

$$
\kappa(\theta) = \theta m_D - \frac{1}{2} r\gamma(\theta^2\sigma_D^2 + 2\rho_h\theta\sigma_D\sigma_\eta),
\tag{4.17}
$$

$$
\bar{\delta} = r\gamma(\rho_l - \rho_h)\sigma_D\sigma_\eta > 0.
\tag{4.18}
$$

A natural benchmark is the limit price associated with vanishing search frictions, characterized as follows.

Proposition 4.3 *If $s < \mu_{hn} + \mu_{ho}$, then, as $\lambda \to \infty$,*

$$
P \to \frac{\kappa(\theta_o) - \kappa(\theta_n)}{r\bar{\theta}}.
\tag{4.19}
$$

In order to compare the equilibrium for this model to that of the baseline model, we substitute the approximation $e^z - 1 \approx z$ into (4,15) and (4.16) to get

$$
0 \approx ra_{lo} - \lambda_u(a_{ho} - a_{lo}) - \lambda\mu_{hn}(P\bar{\theta} - a_{lo} + a_{ln}) - (\kappa(\theta_o) - \theta_o\bar{\delta}),
$$

$$
0 \approx ra_{ln} - \lambda_u(a_{hn} - a_{ln}) - (\kappa(\theta_n) - \theta_n\bar{\delta}),
$$

$$0 \approx ra_{ho} - \lambda_d(a_{lo} - a_{ho}) - \kappa(\theta_o),$$

$$0 \approx ra_{hn} - \lambda_d(a_{ln} - a_{hn}), -\lambda\mu_{lo}(a_{ho} - a_{hn} - P\bar{\theta}) - \kappa(\theta_n),$$

$$P\bar{\theta} \approx (1-q)(a_{lo} - a_{ln}) + q(a_{ho} - a_{hn}).$$

These equations are of the same form as those in section 4.1 for the indirect utilities and asset price of an economy with risk-neutral agents, with dividends at rate $\kappa(\theta_o)$ for large owners and dividends at rate $\kappa(\theta_n)$ for small owners, and with illiquidity costs given by $\bar{\delta}$ of (4.18). In this sense, we can view the baseline model as a risk-neutral approximation of the effect of search illiquidity in a model with risk aversion. The approximation error[2] goes to zero for small agent heterogeneity (that is, small $\rho_l - \rho_h$). Solving for the price P in the associated linear model, we have

$$P = \frac{\kappa(\theta_o) - \kappa(\theta_n)}{r\bar{\theta}} - \frac{\bar{\delta}}{r} \frac{r(1-q) + \lambda_d + \lambda\mu_{lo}(1-q)}{r + \lambda_d + \lambda\mu_{lo}(1-q) + \lambda_u + \lambda\mu_{hn}q}. \qquad (4.20)$$

The price is the sum of the perfect-liquidity price (that for the case of $\lambda = +\infty$) plus an adjustment for illiquidity that can be viewed as the present value of a perpetual stream of risk premia due to search frictions. The illiquidity component depends on the strength of the difference in hedging motives for trade of the two types of agents, in evidence from the factor $\bar{\delta}$ defined by (4.18). One of the counterparties can be viewed as a natural hedger; the other can be viewed as a hedge provider earning a extra risk premium. The illiquidity risk premium need not be increasing in the degree of overall "market risk" exposure of the asset and would be nonzero even if there were no aggregate endowment risk.

Graveline and McBrady (2011) empirically link the size of repo specials in on-the-run treasuries to the motives of financial services firms to hedge their inventories of corporate and mortgage-backed securities. The repo specials, which are reflections of search frictions in the treasury repo market, are shown to be larger when the inventories are larger, and larger when interest-rate volatility is higher, consistent with (4.18).

---

[2] The error introduced by the linearization is in $O((a_{ho} - a_{lo})^2 + (a_{hn} - a_{ln})^2 + (P\bar{\theta} - a_{lo} + a_{ln})^2)$, which by continuity is in $O((\rho_l - \rho_h)^2)$, for a compact parameter space. Hence, if $\rho_l - \rho_h$ is small, the approximation error is of the order $(\rho_l - \rho_h)^2$.

4.4 NUMERICAL EXAMPLE

We consider a numerical illustration for a market with an annual asset turn-over rate of about 50%, which is roughly that of the OTC market for corporate bonds.

Table 4.1 contains the exogenous parameters for the base-case risk-neutral model. Table 4.2 shows the steady-state equilibrium price and fractions of agents of each type. The annual search intensity of $\lambda = 1250$ shown in table 4.1 implies that an agent expects to be in contact with $1250/250 = 5$ agents a day. Given the equilibrium mass of potential buyers, the average time needed to sell is $250 \times (\lambda \mu_{hn})^{-1} = 1.8$ days. The switching intensities λ_u and λ_d mean that a high-type investor remains a high type for an average of 2 years, while an low-preference agent remains the low type for an average of 0.2 year. These intensities imply an annual turnover of $\lambda \mu_{lo} \mu_{hn}/s = 49\%$, which roughly matches the median annual bond turnover of 51.7% reported by Edwards, Harris, and Piwowar (2007). The fraction of investors holding a position is $s = 0.8$, the discount and interest rates are 5%, sellers and buyers have the bargaining power $q = 0.5$, and the illiquidity cost is $\delta = 2.5$, as implied by the risk-aversion parameters discussed below.

Only a small fraction of the asset, $\mu_{lo}/s = 0.0028/0.8 = 0.35\%$ of the total supply, is "misallocated" to low intrinsic types because of search frictions. The equilibrium asset price, 18.38, however, is substantially below the perfect market price of $1/r = 20$, reflecting a significant impact of illiquidity on the price despite the relatively small impact on the asset allocation. Stated differently, we can treat the asset as a bond whose yield (dividend

Table 4.1 Base-case Parameters for the Baseline Pricing Model

λ	λ_u	λ_d	s	r	β	q	δ
1250	5	0.5	0.80	0.05	0.05	0.5	2.5

Table 4.2 Steady-state Masses and Asset Price for the Baseline Model

μ_{ho}	μ_{hn}	μ_{lo}	μ_{ln}	P
0.7972	0.1118	0.0028	0.0882	18.38

Table 4.3 Base-case Parameters for the Model with Risk Aversion

γ	ρ_h	ρ_l	μ_η	σ_η	μ_D	σ_D	Θ	θ_o	θ_n
0.01	−0.5	0.5	10,000	10,000	1	0.5	16,000	20,000	0

rate of 1 divided by price) is $1/18.38 = 5.44\%$ or 44 basis points above the liquid-market yield r. This yield spread is of the order of magnitude of the corporate-bond liquidity spread estimated by Longstaff, Mithal, and Neis (2005) of between 9 and 65 basis points, depending on the specification and reference risk-free rate.

The base-case risk-neutral model specified in table 4.1 corresponds to a model with risk-averse agents with additional parameters given in table 4.3, in the following sense. First, the "illiquidity cost" $\delta = \bar{\delta} = 2.5$ of low intrinsic type is that implied by (4.18) from the hedging costs of the risk-aversion model. Second, the total amount Θ of shares and the investor positions θ_o and θ_n imply the same fraction $s = 0.8$ of the population holding large positions, using (4.12). The investor positions that we adopt for this calibration are realistic in light of the positions adopted by high- and low-type investors in the associated Walrasian (perfect) market with unconstrained trade sizes, which, from calculations shown in Duffie, Gârleanu, and Pedersen (2005), has an equilibrium large-owner position size of 17,818 and a small-owner position size of −2182. Third, the certainty-equivalent dividend rate per share, $(\kappa(\theta_o) - \kappa(\theta_n))/(\theta_o - \theta_n) = 1$, is the same as that of the baseline model. Finally, the mean parameter $\mu_D = 1$ and volatility parameter $\sigma_D = 0.5$ of the asset's risky dividend imply that the standard deviation of yearly returns on the bond is approximately $\sigma_D/P = 2.75\%$.

Figure 4.1 shows how prices increase with liquidity, as measured by the search intensity λ. The graph reflects the fact that as the search intensity λ becomes large, the allocation and price converge to their perfect-market counterparts (propositions 4.1 and 4.3).

Figure 4.2 shows how prices are discounted for search frictions by an amount that depends on the investors' risk aversion. As we vary the risk-aversion parameter γ, we compute both the equilibrium solution of the risk-aversion model and the solution of the associated baseline risk-neutral model obtained by the linearization (4.20), taking $\bar{\delta}$ from (4.18) case by case. We

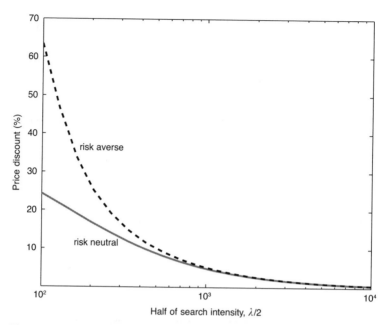

Figure 4.1: Search and illiquidity discounts in asset prices. The graph shows how the proportional price reduction relative to the perfect-market price decreases as a function of the search intensity λ. The solid line plots this illiquidity discount when investors are risk-neutral and may face holding costs that are calibrated to match utility costs in a model with risk-averse investors and time-varying hedging demands, which is illustrated by the dashed line. Source: Duffie, Gârleanu, and Pedersen (2007).

see that the illiquidity discount increases with risk aversion and that the effect is large for our benchmark parameters.

4.5 PRICE RESPONSE TO SUPPLY SHOCKS

So far, we have studied how search frictions affect steady-state prices and returns in a setting in which agents receive idiosyncratic liquidity shocks with no macrouncertainty.

Search frictions affect not only the average levels of asset prices but also the asset market's resilience to aggregate shocks. We examine this by characterizing the impact of aggregate liquidity shocks that simultaneously affect

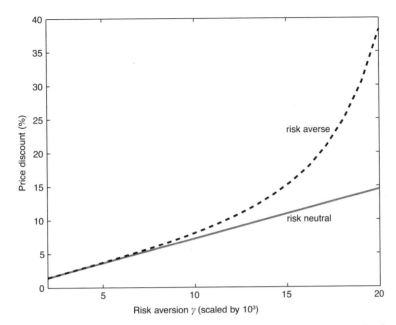

Figure 4.2: Risk aversion and illiquidity discounts. The graph shows the proportional price reduction relative to the perfect-market price, as a function of the investor risk aversion γ. The dashed line corresponds to the model with risk-averse agents, that determined by equations (4.15) and (4.16), while the solid line corresponds to the linearized model, that determined by equation (4.20), in which agents are risk neutral and the holding cost $\bar{\delta}$ and dividend rate κ change with γ. Source: Duffie, Gârleanu, and Pedersen (2007).

many agents. We are interested in the shock's immediate effect on prices, the time pattern of the price recovery, the ex-ante price effect due to the risk of future shocks, and the change in equilibrium search times.

While highly stylized, our model of periods of abnormal expected returns and price momentum following supply shocks also provides additional microeconomic foundations for prior asset-pricing research on "limits to arbitrage" or "good deals," such as described in Shleifer and Vishny (1997) and Cochrane and Saa-Requejo (2001).

We adjust the baseline model in section 4.1 (and, by calibration, the linearized version of the risk-premium model in section 4.3) by introducing occasional, randomly timed, aggregate liquidity shocks. At each such shock, a fraction of the agents, randomly chosen, suffer a sudden "reduction in liquidity," in the sense that their intrinsic types simultaneously jump to the low state. The shocks are timed according to a Poisson arrival process, independent of all other random variables, with mean arrival rate ζ.

Again appealing to the exact law of large numbers, at each aggregate liquidity shock, the distribution μ of agents' intrinsic types jumps to some fixed postshock cross-sectional distribution $\bar{\mu}$ satisfying (4.1) and (4.2) that has an abnormally elevated quantity of illiquid agents, both owners and non-owners. Specifically, $\bar{\mu}_{lo} > \mu_{lo}(t)$ and $\bar{\mu}_{ln} > \mu_{ln}(t)$. Each high-type owner remains a high type with probability $1 - \pi_{ho}(t) = \bar{\mu}_{ho}/\mu_{ho}(t)$ and becomes a low type with probability $\pi_{ho}(t)$. Similarly, a high-type nonowner remains high type with probability $1 - \pi_{hn}(t) = \bar{\mu}_{hn}/\mu_{hn}(t)$ and becomes low type with probability $\pi_{hn}(t)$. Conditional on $\pi(t)$, the changes in types are essentially pairwise-independent across the space of agents. This aggregate "liquidity shock" does not directly affect low-type agents. Of course, the shock affects them indirectly because of the change in the demographics of the market in which they live. By virtue of this specification, the postshock distribution of agents does not depend on any residual "aftereffects" of prior shocks, a simplification without which the model would be relatively intractable.

In order to solve the equilibrium with an aggregate liquidity shock, it is helpful to use the trick of measuring time in terms of the passage of time t since the last shock rather than absolute calendar time. Knowledge of the time at which this shock occurred enables an immediate translation of the solution into calendar time.

We first solve the equilibrium fractions $\mu(t) \in \mathbb{R}^4$ of agents of the four different types. At the time of an aggregate liquidity shock, this type distribution is equal to the postshock distribution $\mu(0) = \bar{\mu}$ (where, to repeat, 0 means zero time units after the shock). After an aggregate liquidity shock, the cross-sectional distribution of agent types evolves according to the ordinary differential equation (4.3), converging (conditional on no additional shocks) to a steady state as the time since the last shock increases.

Given this time-varying equilibrium solution of the type distribution, we turn to the agents' value functions. The indirect utility value $V_\sigma(t)$ depends on the agent's type σ and on the time t since the last aggregate liquidity shock. These values evolve according to

$$\dot{V}_{lo}(t) = rV_{lo}(t) - \lambda_u(V_{ho}(t) - V_{lo}(t)) - \lambda\mu_{hn}(P(t) + V_{ln}(t) - V_{lo}(t))$$
$$- \zeta(V_{lo}(0) - V_{lo}(t)) - (1 - \delta),$$

$$\dot{V}_{ln}(t) = rV_{ln}(t) - \lambda_u(V_{hn}(t) - V_{ln}(t)) - \zeta(V_{ln}(0) - V_{ln}(t)),$$

$$\dot{V}_{ho}(t) = rV_{ho}(t) - \lambda_d(V_{lo}(t) - V_{ho}(t))$$
$$- \zeta((1 - \pi_{ho}(t))V_{ho}(0) + \pi_{ho}(t)V_{lo}(0) - V_{ho}(t)) - 1,$$

$$\dot{V}_{hn}(t) = rV_{hn} - \lambda_d(V_{ln} - V_{hn}) - \lambda\mu_{ho}(V_{ho} - V_{hn} - P)$$
$$- \zeta((1 - \pi_{hn}(t))V_{hn}(0) + \pi_{hn}(t)V_{ln}(0) - V_{hn}),$$

$$P(t) = (V_{lo}(t) - V_{ln}(t))(1 - q) + (V_{ho}(t) - V_{hn}(t))q,$$

where the terms involving ζ capture the risk of an aggregate liquidity shock. This differential equation is linear in the vector $V(t)$, depends on the deterministic evolution of $\mu(t)$, and has the somewhat unusual feature that it depends on the initial value function $V(0)$. Duffie, Gârleanu, Pedersen (2005) solve this system, taking the bargaining power q as exogenous for simplicity rather than incorporating the effects of delay during negotiation that stem from interim changes in the value functions.

4.6 NUMERICAL EXAMPLES

We will illustrate some effects of a liquidity shock with a numerical example and then state some general properties. We assume a search intensity of $\lambda = 250$, that types change idiosyncratically with intensities $\lambda_u = 2$ and $\lambda_d = 0.2$, that the fraction of owners is $s = 0.75$, that the riskless return is $r = 10\%$, that buyers and sellers have equal bargaining powers (that is, $q = 0.5$), that the low-preference-type loss rate is $\delta = 2.5$, that the intensity of an aggregate liquidity shock is $\zeta = 0.1$, and that the postshock distribution of types is determined by $\bar{\mu}_{lo} = 0.377$ and $\bar{\mu}_{ln} = 0.169$. These parameters are consistent with a shock from steady state due to which high types become low types with probability 0.5. The steady-state masses, absent new shocks, are $\mu_{lo} = 0.004$ and $\mu_{ln} = 0.087$.

The price and return dynamics associated with these parameters are shown in figure 4.3 for a scenario in which an aggregate shock occurs at

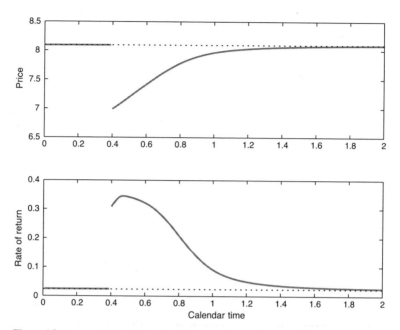

Figure 4.3: Aggregate liquidity shock: effects on prices and returns. The top panel shows the price as a function of time when an aggregate liquidity shock occurs at time 0.4. The bottom panel shows the corresponding annualized realized returns. The liquidity shock leads to a significant price drop followed by a rebound associated with high expected returns. Source: Duffie, Gârleanu, Pedersen (2007).

time 0.4. The top panel of the figure shows prices, and the bottom panel shows realized instantaneous returns for average dividends, both as functions of calendar time.

The rate of return on the asset is computed as the price appreciation rate $\dot{P}(t)$, plus the dividend rate of 1, divided by the price, that is, $(\dot{P}(t)+1)/P(t)$. At time $t = 0.4$, the economy experiences an aggregate liquidity shock, causing the asset price to drop suddenly by about 15%. Notably, it takes more than a year for the asset price to recover to a near-normal level. A buyer able to locate a seller immediately after the shock realizes a relatively high annualized asset return of roughly 30% for several months. While one is led to think in terms of the value to this "vulture" buyer of having retained "excess" liquidity so as to profit at times of aggregate liquidity shocks, our model has only one type of buyer and is therefore too simple to address this sort of vulture specialization.

The large illustrated price impact of a shock is due to the large quantity of sellers and the relatively small quantity of potential buyers that are available immediately after a shock. The roughly 50% reduction in potential buyers that occurred at the illustrated shock increased a seller's expected time to find a potential buyer from 6.2 days immediately before the shock to 12.4 days immediately after the shock. Further, once a seller finds a buyer, the seller's bargaining position is poor because of his reduced outside search options and the buyer's favorable outside options.

Naturally, high-type owners who become low-type owners as a result of the shock experience the largest utility loss.[3] The utility loss for low-type owners is also large because their prospects of selling worsen significantly. High-type owners who do not become low-type owners as a result of the shock are not heavily affected because they anticipate that the market will recover to near-normal conditions before they become low-type owners and wish to sell. (The expected time until one becomes a low-type owner, $1/\lambda_d = 5$, is large relative to the length of the recovery period.) Those high-type agents who don't hold the asset when the shock hits are favorably affected because they stand a good chance of benefiting from the selling pressure.

The prospect of future aggregate liquidity shocks affects prices. For this, we compare the price a "long time after" the last shock (that is, $\lim_{t \to \infty} P(t)$) with the steady-state asset price 9.25 associated with an economy with no aggregate shocks ($\zeta = 0$) but otherwise the same parameters. The presence of aggregate liquidity shocks reduces the price, in this sense, by 12.5%.

The slow price recovery after a shock is the result of two factors: (1) search-based trading illiquidity (captured by λ), and (2) the recovery of individual investors from the shock itself.

The importance of the refinancing channel is reflected by the time, approximately 0.48 year, for the fraction of high-type agents to once again reach $s = 0.75$. This means that, with delayed refinancing and perfect markets, it would take 0.48 years for the price to revert to its normal level. Hence, the additional price sluggishness observed in figure 4.3 is due to search friction.

---

[3] The continuation utilities of the owners drop from $V_{ho} = 9.29$ and $V_{lo} = 9.14$, respectively, to $V_{ho} = 9.24$ and $V_{lo} = 8.47$, while those of the nonowners increase from $V_{hn} = 1.13$ and $V_{ln} = 1.10$ to $V_{hn} = 2.22$ and $V_{ln} = 1.51$.

The implications of these numerical examples seem relatively general. An adverse liquidity shock causes an instantaneous price drop, price momentum during a relatively long recovery period, a reduced long-run price recovery level (due to the risk of future shocks), and an increase in expected selling times. The "time signature" of the price response reflects both the expected time for adversely affected agents to recover, as captured by the parameter λ_u, and the time required for the assets to move from adversely affected sellers to potential buyers, in light of search frictions captured by the parameter λ. The latter effect incorporates both the trading delay due to search and the implications of temporarily superior outside options for potential buyers during negotiation with distressed sellers.

Duffie, Gârleanu, and Pedersen (2007) provide additional characterization of supply shocks in this setting. Feldhütter (2009) estimates a variant of this model by fitting to data on the OTC market for credit default swaps.

CHAPTER 5

Information Percolation in OTC Markets

This chapter describes a simple model of the "percolation" of information of common interest through an OTC market with many agents. Agents encounter each other at random over time and reveal information to each other through bids and offers. We are particularly interested in the evolution over time of the cross-sectional distribution of the posterior probability assignments of the various agents. This chapter is based mainly on results from Duffie and Manso (2007), Duffie, Giroux, and Manso (2010), and Duffie, Malamud, and Manso (2010b).

Hayek (1945) argued that markets allow information that is dispersed in a population to be revealed through prices. The notion of Grossman (1976) of a rational-expectations equilibrium formalizes this idea in a model of a centralized market with price-taking agents. Milgrom (1981), Glosten and Milgrom (1985), Kyle (1985), Pesendorfer and Swinkels (1997), and Reny and Perry (2006) provide alternative strategic foundations for the rational-expectations equilibrium concept in centralized markets. A number of important markets, however, are decentralized. These include OTC markets and private auction markets. Wolinsky (1990), Blouin and Serrano (2001), Duffie and Manso (2007), Golosov, Lorenzoni, and Tsyvinski (2008), Duffie, Giroux, and Manso (2010), and Duffie, Malamud, and Manso (2009, 2010b) study information transmission in decentralized markets.

Models of information percolation are useful in more general settings for social learning. For example, Banerjee and Fudenberg (2004) exploit the exact law of large numbers for random matching among a large population, provide a dynamic rule for updating beliefs, and show conditions for convergence.

The approach taken in this chapter allows a relatively explicit solution for the cross-sectional distribution of posterior beliefs at each time. We begin in the next two sections with the basic information structure for the economy and the setting for search and random matching. We then show how to solve the model for the dynamics of the cross-sectional distribution of information. The remainder of the chapter is devoted to market settings and to extensions of the model that handle public releases of information, the receipt of new private information over time, and the release of information among groups of more than two agents at a time.

5.1 THE BASIC MODEL

A probability space $(\Omega, \mathcal{F}, \mathbb{P})$ and an atomless measure space $(G, \mathcal{G}, \gamma)$ of agents are fixed. The total quantity of agents is $\gamma(G) = 1$.

A random variable X of potential concern to all agents has two possible outcomes, H (high) and L (low), both having nonzero probabilities.

Agents are initially endowed with signals that may be informative about X. Conditional on X, these signals are essentially pairwise-independent (in the sense of appendix A), with outcomes 0 and 1. The probability distributions of signals need not be the same, and the number of signals that an agent receives can vary across agents. For a given signal s_i, we let

$$p_i(k \mid j) = \mathbb{P}(s_i = k \mid X = j),$$

and without loss of generality suppose that $p_i(1 \mid H) \geq p_i(1 \mid L)$. We assume that no signal is endowed to more than one agent.

Conditional on some given signals $s_1, \ldots, s_n$, the logarithm of the likelihood ratio between outcomes H and L is, by Bayes' rule,

$$\log \frac{\mathbb{P}(X = H \mid s_1, \ldots, s_n)}{\mathbb{P}(X = L \mid s_1, \ldots, s_n)} = \log \frac{\mathbb{P}(X = H)}{\mathbb{P}(X = L)} + \theta, \tag{5.1}$$

where

$$\theta = \sum_{i=1}^{n} \log \frac{p_i(s_i \mid H)}{p_i(s_i \mid L)} \tag{5.2}$$

is called the "type" of the signal set $\{s_1, \ldots, s_n\}$. Because the likelihood ratio (5.1) is strictly monotone with respect to the type θ, the conditional probability distribution of X given a collection of signals is completely revealed by the type θ of the signals.

From (5.1), we have the following simple additive rule for updating types as one receives more signals.

Proposition 5.1   *Let $S = \{s_1, \ldots, s_n\}$ and $R = \{r_1, \ldots, r_m\}$ be disjoint sets of signals with types θ and ϕ, respectively. Then $\theta + \phi$ is the type of the combined set $S \cup R$ of signals. Moreover, the distribution of X given $S \cup R$ is the same as the distribution of X given $\{\theta, \phi\}$ or given $\theta + \phi$.*

Because of the market structures that we will consider, only information that is useful in calculating the conditional probability distribution of X is payoff-relevant. We will analyze markets in which the price negotiations between a pair of agents reveal to each of the two agents all the payoff-relevant information associated with their originally endowed signals as well as the payoff-relevant information they have gathered in their prior encounters with other agents. In such a setting, for a given agent α and time t, let $A_0 = \{\alpha\}$, let A_1 denote the set of agents that α has directly encountered before t, let A_2 be the set of agents that those agents had directly encountered before encountering α, and so on. Thus, by time t, agent α holds all the information that was originally endowed to the agents in $A = \cup_{k \geq 0} A_k$. Let S_A denote the union of the signals originally endowed to the agents in A and let θ_A denote the type of the signal set S_A.

For purposes of communicating all payoff-relevant information to each other, the previous proposition implies that it is enough when two agents meet that they merely communicate to each other their current type, or equivalently their posterior probability, given all information received up to the point of their meeting, of the event that $X = H$. We later describe specific market settings in which this complete revelation occurs through bids or offers. While this requires technical conditions, it is natural that, in equilibrium, an agent would bid strictly more for an asset if the posterior probability that that asset pays a high amount is strictly higher.

The previous proposition and induction imply the following result.

Proposition 5.2   *If an agent with extended encounter set A meets an agent with a disjoint extended encounter set B, and if they communicate to each other their posterior probabilities of the event that X is high, then both will hold the same posterior probability of this event as if they had conditioned on the combined set $S_A \cup S_B$ of signals.*

It is convenient to say that an agent with extended encounter set A has type θ_A, which leads to the following equivalent form of the last proposition.

Proposition 5.3 *If an agent whose type is θ meets an agent whose type is ϕ, and if they communicate to each other their types, then both have posterior type $\theta + \phi$.*

5.2 POPULATION INFORMATION DYNAMICS

We now suppose that each agent is matched to other agents at Poisson arrival times with a mean arrival rate (intensity) of λ. At each meeting, the counterparty is randomly selected from the population of agents in the sense described in chapter 3. That is, the probability that the counterparty is chosen from some measurable set A of agents is $\gamma(A)$. We assume that this matching procedure is essentially pairwise-independent across agents, so as to place us in the setting of proposition 5.2, in which any pair of matched agents have disjoint extended encounter sets (almost surely).

Because of the essential pairwise independence of signals after conditioning on X, the initial types of different agents are also essentially pairwise-independent. The exact law of large numbers (theorem A.1 in appendix A) thus implies that, on the event $\{X = H\}$, the fraction of agents whose initial type is no larger than some given number y is almost surely

$$F^H(y) = \int_G 1_{\{\theta_\alpha \leq y\}} \, d\gamma(\alpha) = \int_G \mathbb{P}(\theta_\alpha \leq y \mid X = H) \, d\gamma(\alpha),$$

where θ_α is the initial type of agent α. That is, on the event $\{X = H\}$, the cross-sectional distribution of types over agents is almost surely equal to the average probability distribution of types across agents conditional on $\{X = H\}$. On the event $\{X = L\}$, the cross-sectional distribution function F^L of types is likewise defined and characterized.

For simplicity, we suppose that F^H and F^L have densities, denoted $g^H(\cdot, 0)$, and $g^L(\cdot, 0)$, respectively, and have moment-generating functions that are finite on some open interval containing zero. The differentiability assumption is never actually used but eases the interpretation of the results. For simplicity, we write $g(x, 0)$ for the random variable whose outcome is $g^H(x, 0)$ on the event $\{X = H\}$ and $g^L(x, 0)$ on the event $\{X = L\}$.

We will now provide a calculation of the cross-sectional distribution of types at any time t. We assume, to be verified, that this distribution has a density $g(\cdot, t)$ and moreover that $g(\theta, t)$ is differentiable with respect to t at each type θ. Relying on the exact law of large numbers for continuous-time random matching described in chapter 3, we have almost surely

$$\frac{d}{dt} g(x,t) = -\lambda g(x,t) + \int_{-\infty}^{+\infty} \lambda g(y,t) g(x-y,t)\, dy, \quad x \in \mathbb{R}, \qquad (5.3)$$

which can be written more compactly as

$$\frac{d}{dt} g(t) = -\lambda g(t) + \lambda g(t) * g(t), \qquad (5.4)$$

where $*$ denotes convolution. The first term on the right-hand side of (5.3) is the rate of emigration from type x associated with meeting some agent, becoming more informed, and therefore no longer having type x. The second term is the rate of immigration into type x due to meetings between agents of some type y and agents of type $x - y$, thereby converting the type-y agents to type-x agents because of the additive-in-type property of information sharing stated by proposition 5.3. The convolution integral in this second term is the summation of this immigration rate over all y.

In order to solve (5.3), we will first solve for the Fourier transform of $g(\cdot, t)$ defined by

$$\hat{g}(z,t) = \frac{1}{\sqrt{2\pi}} \int_{-\infty}^{+\infty} e^{-izx} g(x,t)\, dx.$$

From (5.4), for each z in $\mathbb{R}$,

$$\frac{d}{dt} \hat{g}(z,t) = -\lambda \hat{g}(z,t) + \lambda \hat{g}^2(z,t), \qquad (5.5)$$

using the fact that the transform of a convolution $g * h$ is the product $\hat{g}\hat{h}$ of the transforms.

We let $G(z,t) = \hat{g}(z,t)^{-1}$ and use the chain rule to obtain

$$\frac{d}{dt} G(z,t) = \lambda G(z,t) - \lambda,$$

with the usual solution

$$G(z,t) = e^{\lambda t}(G(z,0)-1) + 1.$$

Thus, the differential equation for the transform is solved by

$$\hat{g}(z,t) = \frac{\hat{g}(z,0)}{e^{\lambda t}(1-\hat{g}(z,0)) + \hat{g}(z,0)}. \tag{5.6}$$

We can now invert this transform to get the following explicit solution of the cross-sectional type density $g(\theta,t)$.

Proposition 5.4 *The unique solution of the dynamic equation (5.3) for the cross-sectional type density is the Wild sum*

$$g(\theta,t) = \sum_{n\geq 1} e^{-\lambda t}(1-e^{-\lambda t})^{n-1} g^{*n}(\theta,0), \tag{5.7}$$

where $g^{*n}(\cdot,0)$ is the n-fold convolution of $g(\cdot,0)$ with itself.

The solution (5.7) is justified by noting that the Fourier transform $\hat{g}(z,t)$ can be expanded from (5.6) as

$$\hat{g}(z,t) = \sum_{n\geq 1} e^{-\lambda t}(1-e^{-\lambda t})^{n-1} \hat{g}(z,0)^n,$$

which is the transform of the proposed solution for $g(\cdot,t)$.

A particular agent whose initial type has a probability distribution π_0 at time zero has a posterior type that is a Markov process with a probability distribution π_t at time t that evolves according to

$$\frac{d}{dt}\pi_t = -\lambda\pi_t + \lambda\pi_t * g(t). \tag{5.8}$$

The Fourier transform[1] $\hat{\pi}(t)$ of $\pi(t)$ is therefore given by

$$\hat{\pi}_t(z) = \hat{\pi}_0(z)e^{-\lambda\int_0^t (1-\hat{g}(z,s))\,ds}. \tag{5.9}$$

---

[1] The distribution of a given agent's type cannot have a density because X and the signals have discrete distributions. For a general probability distribution π, a convolution can be defined as $(\pi * g)(x) = \int g(x-y)\,d\pi(y)$, and the Fourier transform is defined as

$$\hat{\pi}(z) = \frac{1}{\sqrt{2\pi}}\int_{-\infty}^{+\infty} e^{-izx}\,d\pi(x).$$

5.3   MARKET SETTINGS

In order to provide specific examples of market settings in which agents have an incentive to completely reveal their information to the agents whom they encounter, we will consider an OTC market in which prices between counterparties are determined by private auctions. At each meeting, agents learn the types of the other agents encountered at that meeting by observing bids submitted in an auction of an asset whose payoff at some future time T depends on X. This bidding information is not revealed to agents that do not participate in the auction. At the payoff date T, X is revealed.

5.3.1   Information Sharing at Wallet Games

Our first of two illustrative market settings, which is extremely simple, leads to information sharing through bids in "wallet games." Uninformed agents that wish to hedge the risk associated with X arrive at the market at a total rate of $\lambda/2$ per unit of time. Any uninformed agent that arrives at the market contacts two informed agents that are randomly chosen from the population of all informed agents.

The uninformed agent conducts a second-price auction with the two chosen informed agents. The lower bidder of the two informed agents sells the uninformed agent a forward financial contract that pays 1 at time T if X is high and 0 otherwise. In return, the contract specifies payment of the winning (low) bid to the informed agent at time T. The bids of the informed agents are revealed only to the two bidders and the uninformed hedger. After purchasing the contract, the uninformed agent leaves the market. Informed agents maximize the expected discounted sum of auction sales net of contract payoffs, with a constant discount factor.

These second-price common-value auctions, known as wallet games, are analyzed by Klemperer (1998). In the unique symmetric Nash equilibrium of each auction, each agent bids his or her posterior probability that $X = H$. From the one-to-one mapping between an agent's type and the agent's posterior probability distribution of X, informed agents learn each others' types from their bids. The dynamics of information transmission are therefore as described in section 5.2. Informed agents earn positive expected payoffs by participating in this market, while uninformed agents earn negative expected profits, consistent with the hedging motive for trade.

Here we have relied on the implication of independent random matching in a continuum population that, when agents meet, they know that in the future they will almost surely not meet again and will not meet someone whose agent contact set directly or indirectly overlaps with their own.

Agents are therefore not strategic about the information they reveal in a meeting. In an OTC market with a finite set of agents, the strategic revelation of information is a complicating concern, as explained by Zhu (2010).

5.3.2 Double Auctions

As a second illustrative market setting, we now consider a special case of the model explored by Duffie, Malamud, and Manso (2010a) in which informed agents buy and sell from each other at double auctions. Suppose that the agents are divided into two intrinsic preference classes, h (high) and ℓ (low). At some time T, the economy ends and the utility realized by an agent of class i for each additional unit of the asset is

$$U_i = v_i 1_{\{X=L\}} + 1_{\{X=H\}},$$

measured in units of consumption, for strictly positive constants v_ℓ and v_h with $v_\ell < v_h < 1$. Upon meeting, a pair of agents participate in a double auction for one unit of the asset. The preference classes of the two agents are observable to each other, and this fact is common knowledge. If the two agents are of the same class, there can be no trade in equilibrium, a result of Serrano-Padial (2007) based on the intuition of the "no-trade theorem" of Milgrom and Stokey (1982). If the agents are of different classes, however, there is scope for trade in equilibrium. The low-preference agent is the potential seller; the high-preference agent is the potential buyer. If the buyer's bid β is higher than the seller's offer σ, trade occurs at the offered price σ. This is sometimes called a "seller's price double auction."

The bid and offer, β and σ, are random variables that depend on (are measurable with respect to) the sets $\mathcal{F}_B$ and $\mathcal{F}_S$ of signals that have been observed by the buyer and seller, respectively, up to the time at which they meet each other. The bid-offer pair (σ, β) constitutes an equilibrium if:

- Fixing β, the offer σ maximizes the seller's conditional expected gain

$$E[(\sigma - E(U_\ell | \mathcal{F}_S \cup \{\beta\}))1_{\{\sigma<\beta\}} | \mathcal{F}_S].$$

- Fixing σ, the bid β maximizes the buyer's conditional expected gain

$$E[(E(U_h | \mathcal{F}_B \cup \{\sigma\}) - \sigma)1_{\{\sigma<\beta\}} | \mathcal{F}_B].$$

As opposed to the symmetric-information setting in chapter 4, the two agents are aware that the asset to be exchanged has a common-value component about which they have received different information. There is a potential for adverse selection, which is more severe for investors with less precise information than that of their counterparties. In order to guard against adverse selection, for example, a buyer may optimally make a conservatively low bid, mitigating the "winner's-curse" risk of purchasing the asset merely because the buyer has not learned adverse information about the asset that is held by the seller. Conservative bidding in the face of adverse selection increases the likelihood that the buyer's bid is less than the seller's offer, thus losing the socially optimal transfer of the asset from the agent that has a lower intrinsic value for owning the asset to the agent with the higher intrinsic value.

Duffie, Malamud, and Manso (2010a) provide a technical condition on the tail of the cross-sectional type densities under which there is a unique equilibrium in which bids and offers are strictly monotone increasing in agents' information types. This equilibrium therefore reveals the types of buyer and seller to each other, implying the solution for information dynamics provided in the previous section. This equilibrium maximizes the probability of trade and is therefore socially optimal among all equilibria. We note that the effective intensity for purposes of modeling the evolution of information is reduced by the likelihood that two randomly matched agents are of the same preference class and therefore have no incentive to engage in bidding and reveal their types to each other. For example, suppose that preference classes are allocated to agents independently of information endowments and that half of the population is of the high-preference class. Then, with a meeting intensity of λ, the intensity of arrival of information-sharing opportunities is $\lambda/2$. More generally, one can solve for the evolution of the cross-sectional type densities of the low-preference class and of the high-preference class, based on a two-dimensional extension of the density evolution equation (5.4).

Duffie, Malamud, and Manso (2010a) also allow classes of agents that differ with respect to initial information quality and search intensity. They focus on the incentives that agents may have to reveal whether they have high or low search intensities, with the implication that those with a low search intensity are likely to have less information and are therefore more exposed to adverse selection. Under some conditions, it is valuable to have a higher meeting intensity, increasing the likelihood of being better informed through trade, provided that one's counterparty is not aware of that informational advantage, but it is preferable to not have this additional information if the counterparty is aware of it because the resulting adverse selection causes the counterparty's bidding behavior to be extremely conservative.

5.4   NUMERICAL EXAMPLE

For a numerical example, we let $\lambda = 1$, so that one unit of time is the mean intercontact time for agents, and we let $\mathbb{P}(X = H) = 1/2$. We assume that each agent α initially observes only one signal s_α and for tractability assume that

$$\mathbb{P}(s_\alpha = 1 \,|\, X = H) + \mathbb{P}(s_\alpha = 1 \,|\, X = L) = 1.$$

We suppose that $\mathbb{P}(s_\alpha = 1 \,|\, X = H)$ has a cross-sectional distribution over the population of investors that is uniform over the interval $[1/2, 1]$. On the event $\{X = H\}$ of a high outcome, this initial allocation of signals induces an initial cross-sectional density of $f(p) = 2p$ for the likelihood $\mathbb{P}(X = H \,|\, s_\alpha)$ of a high state, as illustrated in figure 5.1. The evolution of the cross-sectional distribution of posterior probabilities is calculated from our solution (5.7) of the type density $g(\theta, t)$ and is illustrated in figure 5.1 for various integer times ranging from 1 to 4. As time passes, agents receive more and more information from each other. On the event $\{X = H\}$, figure 5.1 illustrates that the cross-sectional distribution of posterior beliefs places more and more mass, as time passes, closer and closer to the perfect-information distribution, which places all population mass on the posterior probability of 1 for the event $\{X = H\}$. The rate of convergence of the cross-sectional distribution of beliefs to perfect-information beliefs is considered briefly later in this chapter.

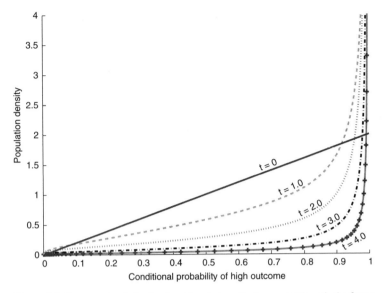

Figure 5.1: Cross-sectional distribution of posteriors. On the event $\{X = H\}$, the figure shows the evolution of the cross-sectional population density of the conditional probabilities held by agents of the event $\{X = H\}$. Source: Duffie, Giroux, and Manso (2010).

Andrei and Cujean (2010) calculate the solution for a richer illustrative example, with an application to the role of price discovery in a centralized trading environment.

5.5 NEW PRIVATE INFORMATION

As an extension of the basic model of information percolation described in section 5.2, suppose that, independently across agents, each agent receives new private signals at Poisson arrivals with an intensity of ρ. Then (5.4) is extended to

$$\frac{d}{dt} g(t) = -(\lambda + \rho) g(t) + \lambda g(t) * g(t) + \rho g(t) * \nu,$$

where ν is the probability distribution of the type of the set of new signals observed at each such event. (For almost every agent, the new-signal type is *iid* across such events.) In this case, the ordinary differential equation (5.5) for the transform $\hat{g}$ is extended to

$$\frac{d}{dt}\hat{g}(z,t) = -(\lambda + \rho)\hat{g}(z,t) + \lambda\hat{g}^2(z,t) + \rho\hat{g}(z,t)\hat{v}(z).$$

We can rewrite this equation as

$$\frac{d}{dt}\hat{g}(z,t) = -\eta(z)\hat{g}(z,t) + \lambda\hat{g}^2(z,t),$$

where $\eta(z) = \lambda + \rho(1 - \hat{v}(z))$. Thus (5.6) is generalized to

$$\hat{g}(z,t) = \frac{\hat{g}(z,0)}{e^{\eta(z)t}(1 - \hat{g}(z,0)) + \hat{g}(z,0)}. \tag{5.10}$$

5.6 MULTIAGENT INFORMATION EXCHANGES

We now extend by allowing a finite number n of agents, not necessarily 2, to share their information at each meeting. For example, suppose that, at Poisson arrivals with an intensity of λ, a given agent is matched with two other agents drawn from the population at random to bid in a double auction for an asset. In this case, $n = 3$. Assuming that bids are strictly monotone in the conditional probability of $\{X = H\}$, (5.3) is extended to

$$\frac{d}{dt}g(x,t) = -\lambda g(x,t) + \lambda \int_{-\infty}^{+\infty}\int_{-\infty}^{+\infty} g(x - y - u, t)g(u,t)g(y,t)\,dy\,du.$$

Letting $w = y + u$, this can be expressed as

$$\frac{d}{dt}g(x,t) = -\lambda g(x,t) + \lambda \int_{-\infty}^{+\infty} g(x - w, t) \int_{-\infty}^{+\infty} g(w - y, t)g(y,t)\,dy\,dw.$$

Letting $r(w,t) = \int_{-\infty}^{+\infty} g(w - y, t)g(y,t)\,dy$, we have

$$\frac{d}{dt}g(x,t) = -\lambda g(x,t) + \lambda \int_{-\infty}^{+\infty} g(x - w, t)r(w,t)\,dw.$$

Now, because $\hat{r}(z,t) = \hat{g}^2(z,t)$, we see that (5.5) is extended to

$$\frac{d}{dt}\hat{g}(z,t) = -\lambda\hat{g}(z,t) + \lambda\hat{g}^3(z,t).$$

More generally, if n agents are drawn at random to exchange information at each encounter, then (5.5) is extended to

$$\frac{d}{dt}\hat{g}(z,t) = -\lambda\hat{g}(z,t) + \lambda\hat{g}^n(z,t). \tag{5.11}$$

In order to solve for $\hat{g}(z,t)$ given $\hat{g}(z,0)$, we let $H(z,t) = \hat{g}(z,t)^{1-n}$. We have

$$\frac{d}{dt}H(z,t) = (n-1)\lambda H(z,t) - (n-1)\lambda,$$

with the usual solution $H(z,t) = e^{(n-1)\lambda t}(H(z,0)-1) + 1$, and

$$\hat{g}(z,t) = H(z,t)^{\frac{1}{1-n}}. \tag{5.12}$$

Extending proposition 5.4, Duffie, Giroux, and Manso (2010) provide an explicit solution for the underlying type distribution in the form of a Wild summation and further extend the model so as to allow a random number of agents at each meeting (independently across pairs of meetings) rather than a fixed number n.

If private information is also learned over time, as in the previous section, then (5.11) is extended to

$$\frac{d}{dt}\hat{g}(z,t) = -(\lambda+\rho)\hat{g}(z,t) + \lambda\hat{g}^n(z,t) + \rho\hat{g}(z,t)\hat{v}(z). \tag{5.13}$$

In this case, we have (5.12), where

$$H(z,t) = e^{(n-1)\eta(z)t}(H(z,0)-1) + 1.$$

5.7 VALID INITIAL TYPE DISTRIBUTIONS

We say that candidates for the initial cross-sectional type density functions $g^H(\cdot,0)$ and $g^L(\cdot,0)$ are *valid* if there exists an initial allocation of signals to agents that imply these initial cross-sectional type densities on the events $\{X=H\}$ and $\{X=L\}$, respectively. Because the two outcomes of the type densities are related to each other through conditioning on signals and then computation of log-likelihood ratios, it is not immediately obvious how one can find a pair of initial density functions $g^H(\cdot,0)$ and $g^L(\cdot,0)$ that are indeed valid. Lemma A.1 in Duffie, Malamud, and Manso (2010a), restated as the following proposition, provides a simple approach to constructing valid initial type distributions.

Proposition 5.5   *A pair* $(g^H(\cdot,0),\ g^L(\cdot,0))$ *of initial cross-sectional type densities is valid if, for any type* x,

$$g^L(x,0) = e^{\{-x\}}g^H(x,0). \tag{5.14}$$

Thus, in order to construct working examples, one could simply take $g^H(\cdot,0)$ to be an *arbitrary* density function and let $g^L(x,0) = e^{\{-x\}}g^H(x,0)$.

5.8   CONVERGENCE AND FURTHER EXTENSIONS

We have shown how the percolation of information through heavily populated markets can be modeled so as to allow a relatively explicit solution for the cross-sectional distribution of posterior beliefs at each time.

In the setting of this chapter, Duffie, Giroux, and Manso (2010) show that (provided the initial distribution of information is nontrivial) the cross-sectional distribution of beliefs converges exponentially to perfect information (almost all agents assign probability 1 to the true outcome of X in the limit). The convergence rate is the meeting intensity λ, irrespective of the number n of agents at each private meeting. Duffie, Malamud, and Manso (2010b) extend this model to allow for releases over time of the private information held by finite sets of agents. The mean arrival rate of these public announcements is some fixed intensity η. They also extend by allowing the number of agents at each meeting to be random, not necessarily a fixed number n. Provided that the mean arrival rate λ of private information sharing is strictly positive, the rate of convergence of the cross-sectional distribution of posterior beliefs is simply $\lambda + \eta$. If, however, $\lambda = 0$, then convergence is at a rate strictly lower than η. In this sense, private information sharing promotes the effect of public information sharing.

Duffie, Malamud, and Manso (2009) consider the endogenous choice of search intensities, with a focus on the equilibrium implications of complementary learning. Individual agents search more intensively for opportunities to gather information if they conjecture that other agents are also searching more intensively because the other agents are in that case more likely to be encountered and also more likely to be well informed. If, however, agents conjecture that other agents are making no effort to search for information-gathering opportunities, then the incentive to search is reduced, in some cases to the point of equilibrium with no learning at all.

APPENDIX A

Foundations for Random Matching

This appendix summarizes conditions from Duffie and Sun (2011) for an exact law of large numbers for random matching of a "continuum" of investors in a static setting. Existence of models satisfying these conditions is shown in Duffie and Sun (2007). These sources also provide Markovian dynamics for agents' type distributions in multiperiod settings.

A.1 MATHEMATICAL PRELIMINARIES

Let $(\Omega, \mathcal{F}, \mathbb{P})$ be a probability space and let $(G, \mathcal{G}, \gamma)$ be an atomless space of agents of total mass $\gamma(G) = 1$. For example, G could be the unit interval $[0, 1]$ with the uniform distribution (Lebesgue measure). Let $(G \times \Omega, \mathcal{G} \otimes \mathcal{F}, \gamma \otimes \mathbb{P})$ be the usual product space. For a function f on $G \times \Omega$ and for some $(i, \omega) \in G \times \Omega$, a function $f_i = f(i, \cdot)$ represents the outcome for agent i across the different states, and the function $f_\omega = f(\cdot, \omega)$ on G represents the cross section of outcomes in state ω for the different agents.

In order to work with independent type processes arising from random matching, we define an extension of the usual measure-theoretic product that retains the Fubini property. A formal definition is as follows.

Definition 1 *A probability space $(G \times \Omega, \mathcal{W}, Q)$ extending the usual product space $(G \times \Omega, \mathcal{G} \otimes \mathcal{F}, \gamma \otimes \mathbb{P})$ is said to be a Fubini extension if, for any real-valued Q-integrable function g on $(G \times \Omega, \mathcal{W})$, the functions $g_i = g(i, \cdot)$ and $g_\omega = g(\cdot, \omega)$ are integrable, respectively, on $(\Omega, \mathcal{F}, \mathbb{P})$ for γ-almost all $i \in i$ and on $(G, \mathcal{G}, \gamma)$ for P-almost all $\omega \in \Omega$; and if, moreover, $\int_\Omega g_i \, d\mathbb{P}$ and $\int_G g_\omega \, d\gamma$ are integrable, respectively, on $(G, \mathcal{G}, \gamma)$ and on $(\Omega, \mathcal{F}, \mathbb{P})$, with $\int_{G \times \Omega} g \, dQ = \int_G \left(\int_\Omega g_i \, d\mathbb{P} \right) d\gamma = \int_\Omega \left(\int_G g_\omega \, d\gamma \right) d\mathbb{P}$.*

From this point, we fix a Fubini extension of $(G \times \Omega, \mathcal{G} \otimes \mathcal{F}, \gamma \otimes \mathbb{P})$ that is denoted $(G \times \Omega, \mathcal{G} \boxtimes \mathcal{F}, \gamma \boxtimes \mathbb{P})$. We introduce an independence condition, taking a complete separable metric space X of outcomes for the sake of generality. For example, finite spaces and Euclidean spaces are complete separable metric spaces.

Definition 2   *An $\mathcal{G} \boxtimes \mathcal{F}$-measurable function f from $G \times \Omega$ to a complete separable metric space X is said to be essentially pairwise-independent if for γ-almost every agent $i \in G$, the random variables f_i and f_j are independent for γ-almost every agent $j \in G$.*

The following version of the exact law of large numbers of Sun (2006) gives a calculation of the almost surely deterministic cross-sectional distribution of a continuum of essentially pairwise-independent random variables.

Theorem A.1   *(exact law of large numbers). Suppose $f : G \times \Omega \to X$ is $\mathcal{G} \boxtimes \mathcal{F}$-measurable and essentially pairwise-independent. Then, almost surely, for any measurable subset A of X,*

$$\int_G 1_{\{f_i \in A\}} \, d\gamma(i) = \int_G \mathbb{P}(f_i \in A) \, d\gamma(i). \tag{A.1}$$

The conclusion (A.1) is that independence implies that the empirical cross-sectional distribution of the random variables coincides almost surely with the average across agents of the probability distributions of the random variables. For example, if the random variables $\{f_i : i \in G\}$ have the same probability distribution with a finite expectation m, then the empirical average is almost surely m.

A.2   RANDOM MATCHING RESULTS

We first define a random full matching for a finite set of types.

Definition 3   *(full matching).*

1. *Let $S = \{1, 2, \ldots, K\}$ be a finite set of types and $\alpha : G \to S$ be a $\mathcal{G}$-measurable function that maps agents to types. Let p denote the*

cross-sectional distribution of types. That is, for each type k and for $G_k = \{i \in G : \alpha(i) = k\}$, *we have* $p_k = \gamma(G_k)$.

2. *A full matching is a bijection ϕ from G to G such that, for each $i \in G$,* $\phi(i) \neq i$ *and* $\phi(\phi(i)) = i$.

3. *A random full matching is a mapping π from $G \times \Omega$ to G such that (i) π_ω is a full matching for each $\omega \in \Omega$; (ii) the associated type mapping $g = \alpha(\pi) : G \times \Omega \to S$ is $\mathcal{G} \boxtimes \mathcal{F}$-measurable; and (iii) for γ-almost every agent $i \in G$, the probability distribution of g_i (the random variable describing the type of the agent to which i is matched), is p.*

4. *A random full matching π is said to be independent in types if the agent-to-type mapping g is essentially pairwise independent.*

Condition 1 of this definition says that a fraction p_k of the population is of type k. Condition 2 says that there is no self-matching and that if i is matched to j, then j is matched to i. Condition 3 *(iii)* means that for almost every agent i, the probability that i is matched to a type-k agent is p_k. Condition 4 says that for almost every pair of agents i and $j \in G$, the event that agent i matched to a type-k agent is independent of the event that agent j matched to a type-l agent, for any k and l in S.

Because agents of type k have a common probability p_l of being matched to type-l agents, the independence condition 4 and the exact law of large numbers imply that the relative fraction of agents matched to type-l agents among the type-k population is almost surely p_l (that is, empirical frequency coincides with probability). This means that the fraction of the total population consisting of type-k agents that are matched to type-l agents is almost surely $p_k p_l$. This result is stated in the following theorem, whose proof is given in Duffie and Sun (2011).

Theorem A.2 *Let $\alpha : G \to S$ be a $\mathcal{G}$-measurable type function with type distribution $p = (p_1, \ldots, p_K)$. If a random full matching π is independent in types, then for any given types k and l,*

$$\gamma(\{i : \alpha(i) = k, \alpha(\pi_\omega(i)) = l\}) = p_k p_l \quad \text{almost surely.} \quad (A.2)$$

The statement is that pairwise-independent matching causes the quantity of type-k agents mapped to type-l agents to be equal to the expected quantity almost surely.

We now consider the case of random partial matchings, starting with the definition.

Definition 4 *(partial matching). Let $\alpha : G \to S$ be a $\mathcal{G}$-measurable type function with type distribution $p = (p_1, \dots, p_K)$. Let π be a mapping from $G \times \Omega$ to $G \cup \{J\}$, where J denotes "no match."*

1. *We say that π is a random partial matching with no-match probabilities $q_1, \dots, q_K$ if (i) for each $\omega \in \Omega$, the restriction of π_ω to the set $M_\omega = \{i : \pi(i) \neq J\}$ of matched agents is a full matching on M_ω; (ii) after extending the type function α to $G \cup \{J\}$ by the assignment $\alpha(J) = J$ and then letting $g = \alpha(\pi)$, g is a $\mathcal{G} \boxtimes \mathcal{F}$-measurable function that assigns each agent to some type or to no-match; (iii) for γ-almost every $i \in G_k$, $\mathbb{P}(g_i = J) = q_k$ and*

$$\mathbb{P}(g_i = l) = \frac{(1-q_k)p_l(1-q_l)}{\sum_{r=1}^{K} p_r(1-q_r)}. \tag{A.3}$$

2. *A random partial matching π is said to be independent in types if the agent-to-type mapping $g = \alpha(\pi)$ is essentially pairwise independent.*

Part (i) of statement 1 means that any agent i with $\pi_\omega(i) = J$ is not matched in state ω, while any other agent is matched. Equation (A.3) is interpreted by noting that if an agent of type k is matched, the probability of being matched to a type-l agent must be proportional to the type distribution of matched agents. The fraction of the population of matched agents among the total population is $\sum_r p_r(1 - q_r)$. Thus the probability that a matched agent's counterparty is a type-l agent is

$$\frac{p_l(1-q_l)}{\sum_{r=1}^{K} p_r(1-q_r)} \quad \text{almost surely.}$$

This implies that the probability that a type-k agent is matched to a type-l agent is given by (A.3). If $\sum_r p_r(1 - q_r) = 0$, we have $p_k(1 - q_k) = 0$ for all $1 \le k \le K$, in which case almost no agents are matched, and we can interpret

$$\frac{(1-q_k)p_l(1-q_l)}{\sum_{r=1}^{K} p_r(1-q_r)}$$

as zero.

The following result of Duffie and Sun (2011) generalizes theorem A.2 to the case of random partial matchings. The existence of models satisfying the stated conditions is shown by Duffie and Sun (2007).

Theorem A.3 *Suppose that π is a random partial matching from $G \times \Omega$ to $G \cup \{J\}$ with no-match probabilities $q_1, \ldots, q_K$. If π is independent in types, then almost surely*

1. *The fraction of the total population consisting of unmatched agents of type k is*

$$\gamma(\{i \in G : \alpha(i) = k, g_i = J\}) = p_k q_k. \tag{A.4}$$

2. *For any types k and l the fraction of the total population consisting of type-k agents that are matched to type-l agents is*

$$\gamma(\{i : \alpha(i) = k, g_i = l\}) = \frac{p_k(1 - q_k)p_l(1 - q_l)}{\sum_{r=1}^{K} p_r(1 - q_r)}. \tag{A.5}$$

APPENDIX B

Counting Processes

This appendix reviews intensity-based models of counting processes. Brémaud (1981) is a standard source.

All properties below are with respect to a probability space $(\Omega, \mathcal{F}, \mathbb{P})$ and a given filtration $\{\mathcal{F}_t : t \geq 0\}$ satisfying the usual conditions unless otherwise indicated. We say that some $X : \Omega \times [0, \infty) \to \mathbb{R}$ is adapted if, for each time t, the function $X(\cdot, t) : \Omega \to \mathbb{R}$, also denoted X_t or $X(t)$, is $\mathcal{F}_t$-measurable. For market applications, $\mathcal{F}_t$ corresponds to the information held by a given set of agents at time t. To say that a process X is adapted can be interpreted as stating that X_t is observable at time t, or could be chosen by agents at time t, on the basis of the information represented by $\mathcal{F}_t$.

A process Y is predictable if $Y : \Omega \times [0, \infty) \to \mathbb{R}$ is measurable with respect to the σ-algebra on $\Omega \times [0, \infty)$ generated by the set of all left-continuous adapted processes. The idea is that one can "foretell" Y_t based on all of the information available up to, but not including, time t. Of course, any left-continuous adapted process is predictable, as is, in particular, any continuous process.

A counting process N is defined via an increasing sequence $\{T_0, T_1, \ldots\}$ of random variables valued in $[0, \infty]$, with $T_0 = 0$ and with $T_n < T_{n+1}$ whenever $T_n < \infty$, according to

$$N_t = n, \quad t \in [T_n, T_{n+1}), \tag{B.1}$$

where we define $N_t = +\infty$ if $t \geq \lim_n T_n$. We may treat T_n as the nth jump time of N, and N_t as the number of jumps that have occurred up to and including time t. The counting process is nonexplosive if $\lim T_n = +\infty$ almost surely.

Definitions of "intensity" vary slightly from place to place. One may refer to section II.3 of Brémaud (1981), in particular theorems T8 and T9, to compare other definitions of intensity with the following. Let λ be a nonnegative predictable process such that, for all t, we have $\int_0^t \lambda_s \, ds < \infty$ almost surely. Then a nonexplosive adapted counting process N has λ as its intensity if $\{N_t - \int_0^t \lambda_s \, ds : t \geq 0\}$ is a local martingale.

From Brémaud's theorem T12, without an important loss of generality for our purposes, we can require an intensity to be predictable, as above, and we can treat an intensity as essentially unique in that: If λ and $\tilde{\lambda}$ are both intensities for N, as defined above, then

$$\int_0^\infty |\lambda_s - \tilde{\lambda}_s| \lambda_s \, ds = 0 \quad \text{almost surely.} \tag{B.2}$$

We note that if λ is strictly positive, then (B.2) implies that $\lambda = \tilde{\lambda}$ almost everywhere.

We can get rid of the annoying "localness" of the above local-martingale characterization of intensity under the following technical condition, which can be verified from theorems T8 and T9 of Brémaud (1981).

Proposition B.1 *Suppose that N is an adapted counting process and λ is a nonnegative predictable process such that, for all t, $E\left(\int_0^t \lambda_s \, ds\right) < \infty$. Then the following are equivalent:*

(i) N is nonexplosive and λ is the intensity of N.
(ii) $\left\{N_t - \int_0^t \lambda_s \, ds : t \geq 0\right\}$ is a martingale.

Proposition B.2 *Suppose that N is a nonexplosive adapted counting process with intensity λ, with $\int_0^t \lambda_s \, ds < \infty$ almost surely for all t. Let M be defined by $M_t = N_t - \int_0^t \lambda_s \, ds$. Then, for any predictable process H such that $\int_0^t |H_s| \lambda_s \, ds$ is finite almost surely for all t, a local martingale Y is well defined by*

$$Y_t = \int_0^t H_s \, dM_s = \int_0^t H_s \, dN_s - \int_0^t H_s \lambda_s \, ds.$$

If, moreover, $E\left[\int_0^t |H_s| \lambda_s \, ds\right] < \infty$ for all t, then Y is a martingale.

In order to define a Poisson process, we first recall that a random variable K with outcomes $\{0, 1, 2, \ldots\}$ has the Poisson distribution with parameter β if

$$\mathbb{P}(K = k) = e^{-\beta} \frac{\beta^k}{k!},$$

noting that $0! = 1$. A Poisson process is an adapted nonexplosive counting process N with deterministic intensity λ such that $\int_0^t \lambda_s \, ds$ is finite almost surely for all t, with the property that, for all t and $s > t$, conditional on $\mathcal{F}_t$, the random variable $N_s - N_t$ has the Poisson distribution with parameter $\int_t^s \lambda_u \, du$. (See Brémaud (1981, p. 22).)

Bibliography

Afonso, G., and R. Lagos, 2011, "Trade Dynamics in the Market for Federal Funds," Working Paper, New York University.

Andrei, D., and J. Cujean, 2010, "Information Percolation in Centralized Markets," Working Paper, University of Lausanne.

Ashcraft, A., and D. Duffie, 2007, "Systemic Illiquidity in the Federal Funds Market," *American Economic Review, Papers and Proceedings*, 97, 221–225.

Atakan, A., and M. Ekmekci, 2010, "Bargaining and Reputation in Search Markets," Working Paper, Northwestern University.

Banerjee, A., and D. Fudenberg, 2004, "Word-of-Mouth Learning," *Games and Economic Behavior*, 46, 1–22.

Bessembinder, H., and W. Maxwell, 2008, "Markets: Transparency and the Corporate Bond Market," *Journal of Economic Perspectives*, 22, 217–234.

Bhattacharya, S., and K. M. Hagerty, 1987, "Dealerships, Trading Externalities, and General Equilibrium," in *Contractual Arrangements for Intertemporal Trade*, ed. by E. Prescott and N. Wallace. Minneapolis: University of Minnesota Press, Minnesota Studies in Macroeconomics Series, vol. 1, pp. 81–104.

Binmore, K., and L. Samuelson, 1999, "Evolutionary Drift and Equilibrium Selection," *Review of Economic Studies*, 66, 363–393.

Blocher, J., A. Reed, and E. Van Wesep, 2010, "Connecting Two Markets: An Equilibrium Framework for Shorts, Longs and Stock Loans," Working Paper, Kenan-Flagler Business School, University of North Carolina at Chapel Hill.

Blouin, M., and R. Serrano, 2001, "A Decentralized Market with Common Values Uncertainty: Non-Steady States," *Review of Economic Studies*, 68, 323–346.

Boni, L., and C. Leach, 2004, "Expandable Limit Order Markets," *Journal of Financial Markets*, 7, 145–185.

Brémaud, P., 1981, *Point Processes and Queues: Martingale Dynamics*. New York: Springer-Verlag.

Burdzy, K., D. M. Frankel, and A. Pauzner, 2001, "Fast Equilibrium Selection by Rational Players Living in a Changing World," *Econometrica*, 69, 163–189.

Cavalli-Sforza, L. L., and W. F. Bodmer, 1971, *The Genetics of Human Population*. San Francisco: Freeman.

Chen, Z., A. A. Lookman, N. Schürhoff, and D. J. Seppi, 2009, "Why Ratings Matter: Evidence from Lehman's Index Rating Rule Change," Working Paper, Carnegie-Mellon University.

Cocco, J., F. Gomes, and N. Martins, 2009, "Lending Relationships in the Interbank Market," *Journal of Financial Intermediation*, 18, 24–48.

Cochrane, J., and J. Saa-Requejo, 2001, "Good-Deal Asset Pricing Bounds in Incomplete Markets," *Journal of Political Economy*, 108, 79–119.

Craig, B., and G. von Peter, 2010, "Interbank Tiering and Money Center Banks," Working Paper, Federal Reserve Bank of Cleveland, Deutsche Bundesbank, and European Business School.

D'Avolio, G., 2002, "The Market for Borrowing Stock," *Journal of Financial Economics*, 66, 271–306.

Dekel, E., and S. Scotchmer, 1999, "On the Evolution of Attitudes towards Risk in Winner-Take-All Games," *Journal of Economic Theory*, 87, 125–143.

Diamond, P., 1971, "A Model of Price Adjustment," *Journal of Economic Theory*, 3, 156–168.

———, 1982, "Aggregate Demand Management in Search Equilibrium," *Journal of Political Economy*, 90, 881–894.

Diamond, P., and J. Yellin, 1990, "Inventories and Money Holdings in a Search Economy," *Econometrica*, 58, 929–950.

Duffie, D., 2010, "Asset Price Dynamics with Slow-Moving Capital," *Journal of Finance*, 65, 1238–1268.

———, 2011, "On the Clearing of Foreign Exchange Derivatives," Graduate School of Business, Stanford University, Submission to the U.S. Treasury.

Duffie, D., N. Gârleanu, and L. H. Pedersen, 2002, "Securties Lending, Shorting, and Pricing," *Journal of Financial Economics*, 66, 307–339.

———, 2005, "Over-the-Counter Markets," *Econometrica*, 73, 1815–1847.

———, 2007, "Valuation in Over-the-Counter Markets," *Review of Financial Studies*, 20, 1865–1900.

Duffie, D., G. Giroux, and G. Manso, 2010, "Information Percolation," *AEJ: Microeconomic Theory*, 2, 100–111.

Duffie, D., and M. Huang, 1996, "Swap Rates and Credit Quality," *Journal of Finance*, 51, 921–950.

Duffie, D., A. Li, and T. Lubke, 2009, "Policy Perspectives on Over-the-Counter Derivatives Market Infrastructure," Staff Report 424, Federal Reserve Bank of New York.

Duffie, D., S. Malamud, and C. Manso, 2009, "Information Percolation with Equilibrium Search Dynamics," *Econometrica*, 77, 1513–1574.

———, 2010a. "Information Percolation in Segmented Markets," Working Paper, Stanford University.

———, 2010b, "The Relative Contributions of Private Information Sharing and Public Information Releases to Information Aggregation," *Journal of Economic Theory*, 145, 1574–1601.

Duffie, D., and G. Manso, 2007, "Information Percolation in Large Markets," *American Economic Review*, Papers and Proceedings, 97, 203–209.

Duffie, D., M. Schroder, and C. Skiadas, 1996, "Recursive Valuation of Defaultable Securities and the Timing of the Resolution of Uncertainty," *Annals of Applied Probability*, 6, 1075–1090.

Duffie, D., and B. Strulovici, 2007, "Capital Mobility and Asset Pricing," Working Paper, Stanford University.

Duffie, D., and Y. Sun, 2007, "Existence of Independent Random Matching," *Annals of Applied Probability*, 17, 386–419.

———, 2011, "The Exact Law of Large Numbers for Independent Random Matching," Working Paper, Stanford University, forthcoming in *Journal of Economic Theory*.

Duffie, D., and H. Zhu, 2011, "Does a Central Clearing Counterparty Reduce Counterparty Risk?" Working Paper, Graduate School of Business, Stanford University, forthcoming in *Review of Asset Pricing Studies*.

Edwards, A. K., L. E. Harris, and M. S. Piwowar, 2007, "Corporate Bond Market Transaction Costs and Transparency," *Journal of Finance*, 62, 1421–1451.

Feldhütter, P., 2009, "The Same Bond at Different Prices: Identifying Search Frictions and Selling Pressures," Working Paper, University of Copenhagen forthcoming in *Review of Financial Studies*.

Ferland, R., and G. Giroux, 2008, "Law of Large Numbers for Dynamic Bargaining Markets," *Journal of Applied Probability*, 45, 45–54.

Froot, K., and P. O'Connell, 1999, "The Pricing of US Catastrophe Reinsurance," in *The Financing of Catastrophe Risk*, ed. by K. Froot. University of Chicago Press, pp. 195–232.

Fudenberg, D., and D. Levine, 1993, "Steady-State Learning and Nash Equilibrium," *Econometrica*, 61, 547–573.

Furfine, C., 2001, "Banks as Monitors of Other Banks, Evidence from the Overnight Federal Funds Market," *Journal of Business*, 74, 33–57.

Gale, D., 1986a, "Bargaining and Competition, Part I: Characterization," *Econometrica*, 54, 785–806.

——, 1986b, "Bargaining and Competition, Part II: Existence," *Econometrica*, 54, 807–818.

Gârleanu, N., 2009, "Pricing and Portfolio Choice in Imperfect Markets," *Journal of Economic Theory*, 144, 532–564.

Geczy, C. C., D. K. Musto, and A. V. Reed, 2002, "Stocks Are Special Too: An Analysis of the Equity Lending Market," *Journal of Financial Economics*, 66, 241–269.

Gehrig, T., 1993, "Intermediation in Search Markets," *Journal of Economics and Management Strategy*, 2, 97–120.

Glosten, L., and P. Milgrom, 1985, "Bid, Ask, and Transaction Prices in a Big Specialist Market with Heterogeneously Informed Trades," *Journal of Financial Economics*, 14, 71–100.

Goldstein, M., E. Hotchkiss, and E. Sirri, 2007, "Transparency and Liquidity: A Controlled Experiment on Corporate Bonds," *Review of Financial Studies*, 20, 235–273.

Golosov, M., G. Lorenzoni, and A. Tsyvinski, 2008, "Decentralized Trading with Private Information," Working Paper, Massachusetts Institute of Technology.

Gravcline, J., and M. McBrady, 2011, "Who Makes On-the-Run Treasuries Special," *Journal of Financial Intermediation*, 20, 620–632.

Green, E. J., and R. Zhou, 2002, "Dynamic Monetary Equilibrium in a Random Matching Economy," *Econometrica*, 70, 929–970.

Green, R., B. Hollifield, and N. Schürhoff, 2007a, "Dealer Intermediation and Price Behavior in the Aftermarket for New Bond Issues," *Journal of Financial Economics*, 86, 643–682.

———, 2007b, "Financial Intermediation in Opaque Markets," *Review of Financial Studies*, 20, 275–314.

Green, R., D. Li, and N. Schürhoff, 2011, "Price Discovery in Illiquid Markets: Do Financial Asset Prices Rise Faster Than They Fall?" *Journal of Finance,* 65, 1669–1702.

Gromb, D., and D. Vayanos, 2007, "Financially Constrained Arbitrage and Cross-Market Contagion," Working Paper, London Business School.

Grossman, S., 1976, "On the Efficiency of Competitive Stock Markets Where Traders Have Diverse Information," *Journal of Finance*, 31, 573–585.

Hamilton, J., 1996, "The Daily Market for Federal Funds," *Journal of Political Economy*, 104, 26–56.

Hardy, G. H., 1908, "Mendelian Proportions in a Mixed Population," *Science*, 28, 49–50.

Harrington, J. E., 1998, "The Social Selection of Flexible and Rigid Agents," *American Economic Review*, 88, 63–82.

Hayek, F., 1945, "The Use of Knowledge in Society," *American Economic Review*, 35, 519–530.

Hellwig, M., 1976, "A Model of Monetary Exchange," Econometric Research Program, Research Memorandum Number 202, Princeton University.

Her Majesty's Treasury, 2009, "Establishing Resolution Arrangements for Investment Banks," London, Her Majesty's Treasury.

Hosios, A., 1990, "On the Efficiency of Matching and Related Models of Search and Unemployment," *Review of Economic Studies*, 57, 279–298.

Hradsky, G. T., and R. D. Long, 1989, "High-Yield Default Losses and the Return Performance of Bankrupt Debt," *Financial Analysts Journal* (July–August 1989), 38–49.

Huang, R., J. Cai, and X. Wang, 2002, "Information-Based Trading in the Treasury Inter-Dealer Broker Market," *Journal of Financial Intermediation*, 11, 269–296.

Johnson, J., 2006, "Consultation Paper on Intraday Liquidity Management and Payment System Policy," Board of Governors of the Federal Reserve System, Docket OP-1257, June 14, 2006.

Keim, D., and A. Madhavan, 1996, "The Upstairs Market for Large-Block Transactions: Analysis and Measurement of Price Effects," *Review of Financial Studies*, 9, 1–36.

Kiyotaki, N., and R. Wright, 1993, "A Search-Theoretic Approach to Monetary Economics," *American Economic Review*, 83, 63–77.

Klemperer, P., 1998, "Auctions with Almost Common Values: The 'Wallet Game' and Its Applications," *European Economic Review*, 42, 757–769.

Krainer, J., and S. LeRoy, 2002, "Equilibrium Valuation of Illiquid Assets," *Economic Theory*, 19, 223–242.

Krishnamurthy, A., and Z. He, 2010, "Intermediary Asset Pricing," Working Paper, Northwestern University.

Kyle, A., 1985, "Continuous Auctions and Insider Trading," *Econometrica*, 53, 1315–1335.

Lacker, J., 2004, "Payment System Disruptions and the Federal Reserve Following September 11, 2001," *Journal of Monetary Economics*, 51, 935–965.

Lagos, R., and G. Rocheteau, 2009, "Liquidity in Asset Markets with Search Frictions," *Econometrica*, 77, 403–426.

Lagos, R., G. Rocheteau, and P.-O. Weill, 2009, "Crises and Liquidity in Over-the-Counter Markets," NBER Working Paper, forthcoming in *Journal of Economic Theory*.

Longstaff, F., S. Mithal, and E. Neis, 2005, "Corporate Yield Spreads: Default Risk or Liquidity? New Evidence from the Credit-Default Swap Market," *Journal of Finance*, 60, 2213–2253.

Lyons, R., 1995, "Tests of Microstructural Hypotheses in the Foreign Exchange Market," *Journal of Financial Economics*, 39, 321–351.

Massa, M., and A. Simonov, 2003, "Reputation and Interdealer Trading: A Microstructure Analysis of the Treasury Bond Market," *Journal of Financial Markets*, 6, 99–141.

McAndrews, J., and S. Potter, 2001, "The Liquidity Effects of the Events of September 11, 2001," *Federal Reserve Bank of New York Economic Policy Review*, 8, 59–79.

McLennan, A., and H. Sonnenschein, 1991, "Sequential Bargaining as a Noncooperative Foundation for Walrasian Equilibrium," *Econometrica*, 59, 1395–1424.

Milgrom, P., 1981, "Rational Expectations, Information Acquisition, and Competitive Bidding," *Econometrica*, 50, 1089–1122.

Milgrom, P., and N. Stokey, 1982, "Information, Trade and Common Knowledge," *Journal of Economic Theory*, 26, 17–27.

Mitchell, M., L. H. Pedersen, and T. Pulvino, 2007, "Slow Moving Capital," *American Economic Review*, Papers and Proceedings, 97, 215–220.

Moresi, S., 1991, "Three Essays in Economic Theory," Ph.D. Thesis, Massachusetts Institute of Technology.

Mortensen, D., 1982, "Property Rights and Efficiency in Mating, Racing, and Related Games," *American Economic Review*, 72, 968–979.

Mortensen, D., and C. Pissarides, 1994, "Job Creation and Job Destruction in the Theory of Unemployment," *Review of Economic Studies*, 61, 397–415.

Newman, Y., and M. Rierson, 2003, "Illiquidity Spillovers: Theory and Evidence from European Telecom Bond Issuance," Working Paper, Graduate School of Business, Stanford University.

O'Hara, M., 1995, *Market Microstructure Theory*. Oxford: Blackwell.

Pancs, R., 2010, "Workup: How Privately Informed Traders (Should) Negotiate over Quantity," Working Paper, University of Rochester.

Pesendorfer, W., and J. Swinkels, 1997, "The Loser's Curse and Information Aggregation in Common Value Auctions," *Econometrica*, 65, 1247–1281.

Porras Prado, M., 2010, "The Price of Prospective Lending: Evidence from Short Sale Constraints," Working Paper, Erasmus University.

Reminik, D., 2009, "Limit Theorems for Individual-Based Models in Economics and Finance," *Stochastic Processes and Their Applications*, 119, 2401–2435.

Reny, P., and M. Perry, 2006, "Toward a Strategic Foundation for Rational Expectations Equilibrium," *Econometrica*, 74, 1231–1269.

Rubinstein, A., 1982, "Perfect Equilibrium in a Bargaining Model," *Econometrica*, 50, 97–109.

Rubinstein, A., and A. Wolinsky, 1985, "Equilibrium in a Market with Sequential Bargaining," *Econometrica*, 53, 1133–1150.

———, 1987, "Middlemen," *Quarterly Journal of Economics*, 102, 581–594.

Serrano-Padial, R., 2007, "On the Possibility of Trade with Pure Common Values under Risk Neutrality," Working Paper, University of Wisconsin-Madison.

Shleifer, A., and R. W. Vishny, 1997, "Limits of Arbitrage," *Journal of Finance*, 52, 35–55.

Soramäki, K., M. Bech, J. Arnold, R. Glass, and W. Beyeler, 2007, "The Topology of Interbank Payment Flows," *Physica A: Statistical Mechanics and Its Applications*, 379, 317–333.

Sorensen, E. H., and T. F. Bollier, 1994, "Pricing Swap Default Risk," *Financial Analysts Journal*, 50(3 (May/June)), 23–33.

Sun, Y. N., 2006, "The Exact Law of Large Numbers via Fubini Extension and Characterization of Insurable Risks," *Journal of Economic Theory*, 126, 31–69.

Trejos, A., and R. Wright, 1995, "Search, Bargaining, Money, and Prices," *Journal of Political Economy*, 103, 118–140.

Tufano, P., 1989, "Financial Innovation and First Mover Advantages," *Journal of Financial Economics*, 25, 213–240.

Vayanos, D., and T. Wang, 2007, "Search and Endogenous Concentration of Liquidity in Asset Markets," *Journal of Economic Theory*, 136, 66–104.

Vayanos, D., and P.-O. Weill, 2008, "A Search-Based Theory of the On-the-Run Phenomenon," *Journal of Finance*, 63, 1351–1389.

Wang, J., 1994, "A Model of Competitive Stock Trading Volume," *Journal of Political Economy*, 102, 127–168.

Weill, P.-O., 2007, "Leaning Against the Wind," *Review of Economic Studies*, 74, 1329–1354.

———, 2008, "The Liquidity Premium in a Dynamic Bargaining Market," *Journal of Economic Theory*, 140, 66–96.

Wolinsky, A., 1990, "Information Revelation in a Market with Pairwise Meetings," *Econometrica*, 58, 1–23.

Yavaş, A., 1996, "Search and Trading in Intermediated Markets," *Journal of Economics and Management Strategy*, 5, 195–216.

Zhu, H., 2010, "Finding a Good Price in Over-the-Counter Markets," Working Paper, Graduate School of Business, Stanford University, forthcoming in *Review of Financial Studies*.

———, 2011, "Do Dark Pools Harm Price Discovery?," Working Paper, Graduate School of Business, Stanford University.

Index